THE ULTIMATE
CHICAGO CUBS
TRIVIA BOOK

A Collection of Amazing Trivia Quizzes
and Fun Facts for Die-Hard Cubs Fans!

Ray Walker

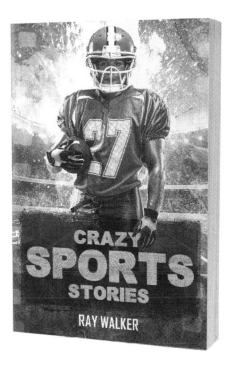

CONTENTS

INTRODUCTION

The Chicago Cubs have been called a lot of things; cursed, crumbling, courageous, Cardinal haters, crosstown rivals, but now, above all — champions. Their 108-year World Series drought was the longest in MLB history. It took them over a century to win their third World Series championship. Yet, they have still been one of the most storied and popular MLB franchises, even during those 108 years.

The Cubs franchise was introduced back in 1876, when they were known as the Chicago White Stockings…yes, essentially the White Sox…I know. This means that, even though they only have three World Series wins under their belts, they still have a long history filled with ups and downs, triumphs and curses.

The Cubs play at Wrigley Field, one of the oldest and most beloved ballparks in the United States. Every baseball fan dreams of seeing that ivy in person at least once in their lives at "The Friendly Confines." The Cubs have Hall-of-Famers like Ernie Banks, Greg Maddux and Fergie Jenkins memorializing their tumultuous yet riveting past. If you're a Cubs fan, the name "Steve Bartman" will give you a chill down your spine and when you see a billy goat, you probably want to scream.

The thing about baseball is that it is a lot like life. There are good times and bad times, good days and bad days, but you have to do your absolute best to never give up. It may take you 108 years, but you can do anything you set your mind to.

When the Cubs won the 2016 World Series, they accomplished something that many did not think they would see happen in their lifetimes. The Cubs made Bill Murray and Eddie Vedder the two happiest men alive that rainy night of Game 7 in Cleveland, along with millions of fans back home.

In 2016, the curse was forever broken and 108 years finally became a thing of the past. The Cubs had become world champions again and had a long past to reflect upon with an optimistic outlook for the future on the North Side of Chicago.

CHAPTER 1:

ORIGINS & HISTORY

QUIZ TIME!

1. Which name has the Cubs franchise NOT gone by in its history?

    a. White Stockings

    b. Orphans

    c. Cats

    d. Colts

2. In what year did the Chicago Cubs franchise make their debut in the National League?

    a. 1901

    b. 1870

    c. 1876

    d. 1955

3. The Chicago Cubs started out as one of the most successful teams in the National League.

    a. True

    b. False

4. Which division do the Cubs currently play in?

    a. American League West
    b. American League Central
    c. National League East
    d. National League Central

5. When did construction on Wrigley Field begin?

    a. 1914
    b. 1995
    c. 1920
    d. 1877

6. Before Wrigley Field was built, where did the Cubs play?

    a. Hilltop Park
    b. West Side Grounds
    c. Shibe Park
    d. Comiskey Park

7. Where did the "Cubs" name originate?

    a. A newspaper nicknamed them the Cubs because of their high number of young players.
    b. Theodore Roosevelt called them the "Cubs."
    c. Owner Albert Spalding wanted to change the team's name.
    d. A bear cub ran across the field during a game.

8. What was Wrigley Field originally named?

    a. Chicago Field
    b. Cubs Park
    c. Comiskey Park
    d. Weeghman Park

4

9. Weeghman Park was actually built for which Federal League baseball team?

    a. Chicago Green Sox
    b. Chicago Whales
    c. Chicago Peppers
    d. Chicago Packers

10. In 1937, the Cubs debuted "W" and "L" flags flown above Wrigley Field to indicate the outcome of the day's game, before mass media coverage. These flags are still in use today. What colors are the "Fly the W!" flags?

    a. Blue and red
    b. Red and black
    c. Blue and white
    d. Red and white

11. Wrigley Field is the second-oldest MLB ballpark in America.

    a. True
    b. False

12. Which song is played after a Cubs win at home over the loudspeaker?

    a. "Go Cubs Go" by Steve Goodman
    b. "It's a Beautiful Day for a Ballgame" by The Harry Simeone Chorale
    c. "Cubs in Five" by The Mountain Goats
    d. "All the Way" by Eddie Vedder

13. Who threw the Cubs' very first no-hitter in 1880?

    a. King Kelly
    b. Tom Poorman
    c. Fred Goldsmith
    d. Larry Corcoran

14. Cubs owner William Wrigley Jr. constructed a ballpark in 1921 to host the Cubs spring training on what island?

    a. Angel Island
    b. Catalina Island
    c. Anacapa Island
    d. Santa Cruz Island

15. The Cubs shared Wrigley Field with the NFL's Chicago Bears for 50 years.

    a. True
    b. False

16. What was the name of the Cubs' official magazine that was around for more than 30 years and discontinued in 2018?

    a. Wrigley Weekly
    b. Cubs Central
    c. Vine Line
    d. Currently Cubs

17. Who suggested planting ivy on the outfield walls of Wrigley Field to make the stadium better resemble a park?

    a. Team president Bill Veeck
    b. Babe Ruth, when he visited Wrigley for the first time
    c. Manager Charlie Grimm
    d. Illinois Governor Henry Horner

18. In 1906, the Cubs won an MLB record ___ games. The Seattle Mariners won the same number of games in the 2001 season.

    a. 122
    b.) 100
    c. 111
    d. 116

    Jackie may

19. Who was the very first manager of the Cubs franchise?

    a.) Hank O'Day
    b. Don Zimmer
    c. Albert Spalding
    d. Bob Ferguson

20. How many World Series have the Cubs won as of the 2019 season?

    a. 2
    b.) 3
    c. 6
    d. 9

13/20

13/20
13/20
8/20
11/20

9/20 6/20 51/100
13/20 9/20
12/20 6/20
7/20 9/20
13/20 11/20
11/20 4/20
10/20

163
340
47.9%

Jackie may 1970 @gmail.

QUIZ ANSWERS

1. C – Cats

2. C – 1876

3. A – True

4. D – National League Central

5. A – 1914

6. B – West Side Grounds

7. A – A newspaper nicknamed them the Cubs because of their high number of young players.

8. D – Weeghman Park

9. B – Chicago Whales

10. C – Blue and White

11. A – True

12. A – "Go Cubs Go" by Steve Goodman

13. D – Larry Corcoran

14. B – Catalina Island

15. A – True

16. C – Vineline

17. A – Team president Bill Veeck

18. D – 116

19. C – Albert Spalding

20. B – 3

DID YOU KNOW?

1. Wrigley Field is named after Bill Wrigley, of chewing gum fame. The Wrigley owned the Cubs from 1921 until 1981 when it was bought by the Tribune Company for $20.5 million.

2. The Cubs first manager, Albert Spalding, was the co-founder of the Spalding sporting goods company. The company began as a store in Chicago in 1876 and became known for manufacturing the first baseball glove and the official baseball of both the American and National Leagues.

3. If the ball lands and gets stuck in the outfield ivy at Wrigley Field, it is a ground-rule double, which means the batter automatically goes to second base.

4. "Hey Hey" was the home run call that former Cubs broadcaster Jack Brickhouse used during games. This is forever memorialized on Wrigley Field's foul poles, which have "Hey Hey" written on them.

5. Three MLB All-Star Games have been hosted at Wrigley Field so far. They took place in 1947, 1962 and 1990. The American League won all three of these games.

6. Former United States President Ronald Reagan did radio recreations of Cubs games for an Iowa radio station in the 1930s.

7. It is pretty well-known that it took a long while for the Cubs to install lights at Wrigley Field. This was because owner P.K. Wrigley donated the original fixtures to aid in the war effort. He made the donation the day after the Japanese attack on Pearl Harbor on December 7, 1941.

8. The Cubs first official night game at Wrigley Field was rained out in the fourth inning. So technically, the Cubs' first complete night game was actually played on August 9, 1988.

9. No Cubs pitcher has ever thrown a perfect game, so far. They have thrown 15 no-hitters in franchise history.

10. There is a sign on a building in right field that reads "EAMUS CATULI!" which translates to "GO CUBS!" from Latin.

CHAPTER 2:

JERSEYS & NUMBERS

QUIZ TIME!

1. The Cubs do not wear numbers on their uniforms, to this day.

    a. True
    b. False

2. How many uniform numbers have the Cubs retired as of the 2019 season (not counting No. 42)?

    a. 8
    b. 12
    c. 5
    d. 3

3. The Chicago Cubs added green briefly to their socks and shoes in 1918.

    a. True
    b. False

4. What did the first Cubs logo look like?

    a. A simple, old English letter "C"
    b. A bear arching its body in the shape of a "C"
    c. The same "C" logo with a bear inside that we see in use today
    d. The word "Cubs" with a bear eating the letter "s"

5. In what year did the Cubs adopt the uniform that fans are used to seeing today? (Pinstripes with the red and blue, circular Cubs logo.)

    a. 1902
    b. 1995
    c. 1969
    d. 1957

6. Who is the latest Cub to have his number retired?

    a. Greg Maddux
    b. Ernie Banks
    c. Ferguson Jenkins
    d. Both A and C

7. The Cubs have a rule that their players are forbidden to wear white socks during games, due to their town rival being the Chicago White Sox.

    a. True
    b. False

8. Whose No. 10 is retired for the Cubs?

    a. Ernie Banks
    b. Ron Santo

c. Billy Williams

d. Greg Maddux

9. Which Cub had the best-selling Cubs jersey in 2019? He also made the list of the Top 15 Best-Selling MLB Jerseys of 2019, coming in at No. 7 after Clayton Kershaw of the Los Angeles Dodgers.

a. Anthony Rizzo

b. Kris Bryant

c. David Ross

d. Javier Báez

10. The Cubs debuted powder blue uniforms for two seasons in 1941 and 1942.

a. True

b. False

11. In 1940, the Cubs wore tank top vest jerseys that closed with _____.

a. A zipper

b. Buttons

c. Velcro

d. Snaps

12. In 1972, the Cubs suffered a manufacturer's error, where their numbers were centered on the front of their uniforms. They are the only team in MLB history to have a centered number on the front of their jerseys.

a. True

b. False

13. The Cubs wore bronze-trimmed jerseys in their 2017 home opener game to commemorate their historic 2016 World Series win.

    a. True
    b. False

14. What number did Sammy Sosa wear as a Cub?

    a. 25
    b. 3
    c. 10
    d. 21

15. What year were numbers added to the front of Cubs road jerseys for the first time?

    a. 1988
    b. 1975
    c. 1957
    d. 1969

16. In 1972, the Cubs wore pants called "Sansabelt" pants. They were pants that had elastic waistbands, which eliminated the need for belts.

    a. True
    b. False

17. During the 2015 season, every Cubs player wore No. 14 patches to honor Ernie Banks.

    a. True
    b. False

18. What are the Cubs official colors?

    a. Midnight navy blue, white and cherry red

    b. Forest green, eggplant purple and white

    c. Wedding gown white, baby blue and Persian red

    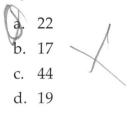d. Air Force blue, Persian red and white

19. What number does current Cubs third baseman Kris Bryant wear?

    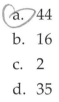a. 22

    b. 17

    c. 44

    d. 19

20. What number does current Cubs first baseman, Anthony Rizzo wear?

    a. 44

    b. 16

    c. 2

    d. 35

QUIZ ANSWERS

1. B – False

2. C – 5

3. A – True

4. A – A simple, old English letter 'C'

5. D- 1957

6. D – Both A and C

7. B – False

8. B – Ron Santo

9. A – Anthony Rizzo

10. A – True

11. A – A zipper

12. A – True

13. B – False, gold-trimmed

14. D – 21

15. D – 1969

16. A – True

17. A – True

18. D – Air Force blue, Persian red and white

19. B – 17

20. A – 44

DID YOU KNOW?

1. The Cubs were one of the first MLB teams to implement the iconic baseball uniform look of pinstripes. The New York Yankees, Boston Braves and Brooklyn Dodgers were some of the others to first wear pinstripes. The Cubs debuted this look in the 1907 World Series.

2. The Cubs have retired five numbers overall and six players overall (two players wore the same number). They are: #10 Ron Santo, #14 Ernie Banks, #23 Ryne Sandberg, #26 Billy Williams, #31 Greg Maddux and Fergie Jenkins. Of course, #42 can also not be worn by any Cubs player. No. 42 is retired throughout all of MLB to honor Jackie Robinson breaking the color barrier in Major League Baseball in 1947.

3. From 1900 through 1905, the Cubs wore uniforms with front pockets on the left breast. A few other teams did this as well. There wasn't really a reason for it. It wasn't for batting gloves, though, that's for sure … because they didn't exist yet.

4. From 1978 through 1981 the Cubs took their interesting powder blue look even further by adding white reverse pinstripes. Many fans call these the Cubs "Pajamas" uniforms.

5. In 1990, the Cubs restored their uniforms to more traditional looks by using jerseys with buttons and belts for pants.

6. The Cub logo featuring a bear has evolved over time. At first, it was a very cute, cuddly-looking bear cub, but it has changed to be a bit more ferocious and daunting to opposing teams.

7. The Cubs were ironically first named the "White Stockings," their current crosstown rivals are the Chicago White Sox.

8. In the 1910s, the Cubs had a logo that included a bear cub sitting in a letter "C" holding a baseball bat.

9. In the 1910s, many Cubs players wore their belt buckle on the side of their leg to avoid injury when sliding into base.

10. Many MLB team road jerseys only display the name of the place the team is from. Only a few include both their location and their team name. The Cubs are one of them who displayed both on a road uniform in the 1930s. These uniforms said "Chicago" across the chest and "Cubs" on the sleeve.

CHAPTER 3:

FAMOUS QUOTES

QUIZ TIME!

1. Which beloved Cub used to always say, "It's a beautiful day for a ballgame. Let's play two"?

    a. Ernie Banks
    b. Sammy Sosa
    c. Ferguson Jenkins
    d. Ryne Sandberg

2. Former Cubs manager Joe Maddon is known for his "Maddonisms." He is known to take part in crazy antics and say crazy things. Which of the below is NOT a Joe Maddon quote?

    a. "Try not to suck."
    b. "If it looks sexy, wear it."
    c. "The future ain't what it used to be."
    d. "Trends can be so trendy."

3. Which former First Lady of the United States is quoted as saying: "Being a Cubs fan prepares you for life – and Washington."?

   a. Michelle Obama
   b. Laura Bush
   c. Nancy Reagan
   d. Hillary Clinton

4. Which former Cubs player said, "Every player should be accorded the privilege of at least one season with the Chicago Cubs. That's baseball as it should be played – in God's own sunshine. And that's really living."

   a. Jon Lester
   b. Alvin Dark
   c. Don Kessinger
   d. Alfonso Soriano

5. Which famous actor said, "Dreams do come true!" after the Cubs won the World Series in 2016?

   a. Vince Vaughn
   b. John Cusack
   c. Bill Murray
   d. Jeremy Piven

6. Ron Swanson, one of the most popular TV characters on the show *Parks and Rec*, once said. "There has never been a sadness that can't be cured by breakfast food." Ron Swanson was played by which real-life Cubs fanatic?

   a. Chris Pratt
   b. Nick Offerman

c. Adam Scott

d. Rob Lowe

7. Which current Cubs player once said, "Every day, there is something new you are working on. It is a challenge every day and that is what makes this game so great"?

   a. Anthony Rizzo

   b. Kris Bryant

   c. Willson Contreras

   d. Kyle Schwarber

8. Sammy Sosa is quoted as saying, "Baseball is the only field of endeavor where a man can succeed three times out of ten and be considered a good performer."

   a. True

   b. False

9. Which famous baseball player is quoted as saying, "You know what God told the Cubs? Don't do anything until I come back"?

   a. Reggie Jackson

   b. Babe Ruth

   c. Cal Ripken Jr.

   d. Pete Rose

10. Cub's broadcaster Harry Caray had a signature phrase during ballgames to help him avoid spewing profanity. That signature phrase was: "Holy ____!"

   a. Cow

   b. Cannoli

c. Cubbies

d. Fudge

11. Which late-night talk show host once said: "I didn't realize it was October until I saw the Cubs choking"?

    a. Jimmy Fallon

    b. James Corden

    c. Conan O'Brien

    d. Jay Leno

12. "Hey, kid! How'd you like to play for the Chicago Cubs?" "Great! But I gotta ask my mom first." This quote is from which movie featuring the Chicago Cubs?

    a. *Fever Pitch*

    b. *Moneyball*

    c. *Rookie of the Year*

    d. *The Rookie*

13. "When we were younger, we used to call him 'Silk,' because he was so smooth with everything he did." – Bryce Harper. Which current Cubs player was Harper talking about?

    a. Anthony Rizzo

    b. Javier Báez

    c. Kyle Schwarber

    d. Kris Bryant

14. When told that Pedro Martinez and Randy Johnson would be making more money than him, which former Cubs pitcher jokingly said: "Oh poor me. What do I do now?! I guess I'll have to get a second job"?

a. Jake Arrieta
b. Greg Maddux
c. Ryan Dempster
d. John Lackey

15. Which Cubs front office executive is quoted as saying, "I just saw over the years that the times that we did remarkable things, it was always because players didn't want to let each other down. Players wanted to lift each other up"?

a. Jim Frey
b. Jed Hoyer
c. Theo Epstein
d. Billy Williams

16. Former Cubs manager Don Baylor once said, "Never allow the fear of striking out keep you from playing the game."

a. True
b. False

17. Current Cubs third baseman Kris Bryant once said, "Make sure your worst enemy doesn't live between your _____."

a. Ears
b. Toes
c. Eyes
d. Fingers

18. Which former Cubs manager said, "Everybody knows something, and nobody knows everything."?

    a. Lou Piniella
    b. Rick Renteria
    c. Rene Lachemann
    d. Dusty Baker

19. What phrase is quoted and engraved on the Chicago Cubs 2016 World Series rings?

    a. "Go Cubs Go"
    b. "We Never Quit"
    c. "Try Not to Suck"
    d. "Champs 4 Life"

20. When Joe Maddon departed the Cubs manager position, Anthony Rizzo was quoted as saying, "I love him like a dad."

    a. True
    b. False

QUIZ ANSWERS

1. A – Ernie Banks

2. C – "The future ain't what it used to be."

3. D – Hillary Clinton

4. B – Alvin Dark

5. C – Bill Murray

6. B – Nick Offerman

7. A – Anthony Rizzo

8. B – False, Ted Williams

9. D – Pete Rose

10. A – Cow

11. D – Jay Leno

12. C – *Rookie of the Year*

13. D – Kris Bryant

14. B – Greg Maddux

15. C – Theo Epstein

16. B – False, Babe Ruth

17. A – Ears

18. D – Dusty Baker

19. B – "We Never Quit"

20. A – True

DID YOU KNOW?

1. "If you have a bad day in baseball, and start thinking about it, you will have 10 more." – Sammy Sosa

2. "You can have all the talent in the world, it's not gonna get you through … It's what you have in your heart." – Ron Santo

3. "The measure of a man is in the lives he's touched." – Ernie Banks

4. "I was taught you never, ever disrespect your opponent or your teammates or your organization or your manager, and never, ever your uniform." – Ryne Sandberg

5. "Mental attitude and concentration are the keys to pitching." – Fergie Jenkins

6. "Statistics are like bikinis – they show a lot, but not everything." – Former Cubs manager Lou Piniella

7. "What you lack in talent can be made up with desire, hustle, and giving 110 percent all the time." – Former Cubs manager Don Zimmer

8. "Don't let anyone say that it's just a game. For I've seen other teams, and it's never the same. When you're born in Chicago, you're blessed and you're healed, The first time you walk into Wrigley Field." Excerpt from the song, "All the Way," by lifelong Cubs fan Eddie Vedder

9. Bob Newhart has been a Cubs fan his whole life. He was

born 21 years after their last World Series win. When they finally won in 2016, he simply said, "You never give up."

10. "Hey batter batter batter! Swing batter! He can't hit, he can't hit, he can't hit, SWING batter!" – Cameron Frey in *Ferris Bueller's Day Off* while attending a game at Wrigley Field with Ferris and Sloane

CHAPTER 4:

CATCHY NICKNAMES

QUIZ TIME!

1. Which former Cub was nicknamed "Grandpa" by his fellow teammates?

   a. Jamie Moyer
   b. Greg Maddux
   c. David Ross
   d. Sammy Sosa

2. Former Cubs manager Joe Maddon gave his RV a nickname. That nickname is "Cousin Eddie."

   a. True
   b. False

3. What was Cubs Hall of Fame pitcher Greg Maddux's nickname?

   a. Pitching Machine
   b. Mad Dog
   c. Maddie
   d. Mad Cub

4. Which former Cubs legend is nicknamed "Mr. Cub?"

   a. Ryne Sandberg
   b. Greg Maddux
   c. Sammy Sosa
   d. Ernie Banks

5. Which is NOT a nickname the Cubs as a team are commonly referred to as?

   a. The Cubbies
   b. The North Siders
   c. The Loveable Losers
   d. The South Siders

6. Javier Báez goes by a nickname in Spanish. What is it?

   a. El Mejor (The Best)
   b. El Rey (The King)
   c. El Mago (The Magician)
   d. El Hechicero (The Sorcerer)

7. From 2001-2002, the Cubs had a player on their team named Fred McGriff, whose last name sounds just like the cartoon character, McGruff the Crime Dog. His nickname was "The Crime Dog" because of this coincidence.

   a. True
   b. False

8. Mordecai Brown only had four and a half fingers, and only three were visible. What was his nickname?

   a. Tri-Fingers
   b. Three-Finger

c. Four-Finger Brown

d. Four and a Half Mord

9. During 2019's MLB Player Weekend, what nickname did Cubs first baseman Anthony Rizzo have displayed on the back of his jersey?

a. Ant

b. For Shizzo, Rizzo

c. Rizzy

d. Tony

10. Which former Cub was nicknamed "The Hawk" because of the way he "attacked the baseball like a hawk"?

a. Andre Dawson

b. Dave Martinez

c. Rafael Palmeiro

d. Ryne Sandberg

11. "Goose" is a nickname. What is former Cubs pitcher Goose Gossage's real name?

a. Maxwell William

b. Richard Michael

c. Kevin Arthur

d. Bartholomew Robert

12. Former Cub Mitch Williams went by the nickname "Wild Thing" but it had nothing to do with the movie *Major League.* The nickname came about because of his wild pitching delivery.

a. True

b. False

13. Cubs first baseman Anthony Rizzo and Cubs third baseman Kris Bryant have quite the bromance. What is their combined nickname?

    a. Krant
    b. Bryzzo
    c. Rizzant
    d. AntKris

14. What is former Cubs pitcher Derek Holland's nickname?

    a. Holly
    b. Dutch Oven
    c. Dutch Derek
    d. Daunting Derek

15. "Sammy" is a nickname in itself for "Samuel," but what other nickname did Sammy Sosa go by during his MLB career?

    a. So Gone Sosa
    b. Right Field Sam
    c. Slammer Sosa
    d. Slammin' Sammy

16. What was Cubs legend Ferguson Jenkins' nickname?

    a. Fergie
    b. Fergilicious
    c. The Ferg Man
    d. Joyful Jenkins

17. Cubs pitcher Kyle Hendricks goes by the nickname "86-Mile Kyle" because his average fastball velocity speed is 86 mph.

    a. True
    b. False

18. Which fictional character nickname did former Cubs manager Don Zimmer go by?

    a. Bugs
    b. Homer
    c. Popeye
    d. Goofy

19. During 2019's MLB Player Weekend, what nickname did Cubs Left Fielder, Kyle Schwarber have displayed on the back of his jersey?

    a. Schwarbs
    b. Schwarby
    c. Left Field Kyle
    d. Krazy Bat Kyle

20. Former Cubs pitcher Rick Sutcliffe went by the nickname, "The Red Baron," due to his ability to cut down opposing batters like a fighter pilot takes down enemies.

    a. True
    b. False

QUIZ ANSWERS

1. C – David Ross

2. A – True

3. B – Mad Dog

4. D – Ernie Banks

5. D – The Southsiders

6. C – El Mago (The Magician)

7. A – True

8. B – Three-Finger

9. D – Tony

10. A – Andre Dawson

11. B – Richard Michael

12. Λ – True

13. B – Bryzzo

14. B – Dutch Oven

15. D – Slammin' Sosa

16. A – Fergie

17. B – False

18. C – Popeye

19. A – Schwarbs

20. B- False

DID YOU KNOW?

1. Former Cubs outfielder Gary Matthews Sr. went by the nickname "Sarge" due to his veteran presence and his role as a leader on the team. His tenure with the Cubs left an impact that was immense both on and off the field.

2. Kyle Hendricks goes by the nickname "The Professor" because he went to Dartmouth and graduated with a degree in economics. His dominant pitching adds to the nickname as well.

3. David Ross is now the Cubs manager. Instead of "Grandpa Rossy," the team will have to start calling him "Skip."

4. Former Cubs manager Joe Maddon goes by the nickname, "Broad Street Joe."

5. Henry Blanco became a Cubs fan favorite in 2005. He went by the nickname "Henry White." Blanco means "white" in Spanish.

6. Wrigley Field's nickname is "The Friendly Confines" because of the fun and exciting atmosphere at the ballpark.

7. The 1989 Chicago Cubs were nicknamed "The Boys of Zimmer" due to making the playoffs and being managed by Don Zimmer. (The nickname is a play on the title of a famous baseball book, *The Boys of Summer*.)

8. Former Cubs second baseman, Ryne Sandberg went by the simple nickname "Ryno."

9. Former Cubs pitcher Aroldis Chapman goes by the nickname "The Cuban Missile" due to his ethnicity and his incredibly fast pitching speeds.

10. During Player's Weekend in 2019, Cubs third baseman, Kris Bryant went by the simple nickname of "KB."

CHAPTER 5:

BRYZZO

QUIZ TIME!

1. Where did Anthony Rizzo go to college?

    a. Florida Atlantic University

    b. UC Berkeley

    c. University of Wisconsin-Madison

    d. He was drafted out of high school

2. The company that Bryant and Rizzo run in their famous MLB commercials is called the *Bryzzo Souvenir Company*.

    a. True

    b. False

3. Anthony Rizzo has a charity foundation that helps cancer patients and their families. What is his charity called?

    a. Cubs Say No to Cancer Foundation

    b. Strike Out Cancer Foundation

    c. The Rizzo Foundation

    d. Anthony Rizzo Family Foundation

4. Anthony Rizzo and Kris Bryant have appeared in the same number of MLB All-Star Games so far in their careers. How many times has each of them been named a National League All-Star (as of 2020)?

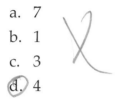

   a. 7
   b. 1
   c. 3
   d. 4

5. Anthony Rizzo and Kris Bryant attended the same elementary school.

   a. True
   b. False

6. How many Gold Glove Awards does Anthony Rizzo have?

   a. 3
   b. 1
   c. 5
   d. 8

7. Where did Kris Bryant go to college?

   a. UC San Diego
   b. San Diego State University
   c. UNLV
   d. University of San Diego

8. Which team did Anthony Rizzo play for in the 2013 World Baseball Classic?

   a. United States
   b. Canada

c. Australia

d. Italy

9. What year did Kris Bryant win the National League Rookie of the Year Award?

   a. 2012
   b. 2014
   c. 2015
   d. 2016

10. What other MLB team did Anthony Rizzo previously play for, before he was traded to the Cubs?

   a. Arizona Diamondbacks
   b. San Diego Padres
   c. Miami Marlins
   d. Toronto Blue Jays

11. Who was Kris Bryant's favorite baseball player when he was growing up?

   a. Mike Piazza
   b. Derek Jeter
   c. Barry Bonds
   d. Tony Gwynn

12. Kris Bryant's favorite cereal is Honey Bunches of Oats.

   a. True
   b. False

13. Who was Anthony Rizzo's favorite baseball player when he was growing up?

a. Mike Piazza
b. Derek Jeter
c. Barry Bonds
d. Tony Gwynn

14. Derek Jeter has his own publishing company under Simon and Schuster called "Jeter Publishing"

a. True
b. False

15. Which fast food restaurant is Anthony Rizzo's favorite?

a. In-N-Out
b. Wendy's
c. Chick-fil-A
d. Taco Bell

16. In which season did both Kris Bryant and Anthony Rizzo participate in the MLB All-Star Home Run Derby?

a. 2015 in Cincinnati
b. 2016 in San Diego
c. 2017 in Miami
d. 2018 in Washington, D.C.

17. The baseball field at Anthony Rizzo's alma mater, Marjory Stoneman Douglas High School, is named "*Anthony Rizzo Field.*"

a. True
b. False

18. What is both Anthony Rizzo's AND Kris Bryant's biggest fear?

a. Spiders
b. Birds
c. Flying
d. Heights

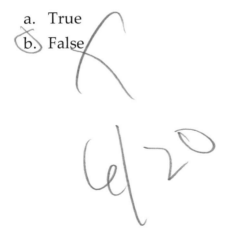

19. What is Kris Bryant's favorite holiday?

    a. Halloween
    b. Christmas
    c. Thanksgiving
    d. St. Patrick's Day

20. Kris Bryant was a groomsman in Anthony Rizzo's wedding and vice versa.

    a. True
    b. False

QUIZ ANSWERS

1. D – He was drafted out of high school

2. A – True

3. D – Anthony Rizzo Family Foundation

4. C – 3

5. B – False

6. A – 3

7. D – University of San Diego

8. D – Italy

9. C – 2015

10. B – San Diego Padres

11. C – Barry Bonds

12. A – True

13. B – Derek Jeter

14. A – True

15. D – Taco Bell

16. A – 2015 in Cincinnati

17. A – True

18. C – Flying

19. B – Christmas

20. A – True

DID YOU KNOW?

1. Kris Bryant married his high school sweetheart, Jessica, in 2017. In April of 2020, they had a son named Kyler. Anthony Rizzo married his wife, Emily in 2018. The two met in Arizona while Rizzo was there for 2016 Cubs spring training.

2. Both Rizzo and Bryant are big advocates of ending gun violence. In Bryant's hometown of Las Vegas, there was a mass shooting at a music festival in 2017. At Rizzo's alma mater, Marjory Stoneman Douglas High School, there was a mass shooting in 2018. Rizzo did give a speech to the students at his former school at a vigil after the incident occurred.

3. Rizzo has a dachshund named Kevin and Bryant has a black cat named Wrigley. Wonder where Kris got the name idea?

4. Kris' dad, Mike threw to him in the Home Run Derby. Rizzo's pitcher for the same Home Run Derby was Cubs coach Franklin Font.

5. In 2016, Kris Bryant became only the second National League player all-time to be named the Rookie of the Year and MVP in consecutive seasons. The feat has been accomplished twice in the American League.

6. The Chainsmokers are Anthony Rizzo's favorite musicians.

7. One of Rizzo's biggest pet peeves is having to share deodorant. Bryant's is when things are not straight or aligned.

8. Math was Rizzo's least favorite subject and the subject he was the worst at while in school.

9. The Anthony Rizzo Family Foundation sold a limited-edition cereal called "RizzO's" to help raise funds for cancer research. The cereal was a honey nut-flavored cereal with an illustration of Rizzo himself gracing the box.

10. Kris Bryant prefers to watch romantic comedies over scary movies.

CHAPTER 6:

STATISTICALLY SPEAKING

QUIZ TIME!

1. Sammy Sosa holds the Chicago Cubs franchise record for the most home runs. How many did he hit?

    a. 601
    b. 545
    c. 555
    d. 501

2. Charlie Root has the most wins in Chicago Cubs franchise history with 201.

    a. True
    b. False

3. How many times have the Cubs made the playoffs?

    a. 10 times
    b. 18 times
    c. 27 times
    d. 20 times

4. Which former Cub comes first in ERA in franchise history at 1.78?

   a. Orval Overall
   b. Hippo Vaughn
   c. Al Spalding
   d. Larry Corcoran

5. Which pitcher has the most strikeouts in Cubs franchise history with 2,038?

   a. Fergie Jenkins
   b. Carlos Zambrano
   c. Charlie Root
   d. Rick Reuschel

6. Which player has the most RBI in Cubs franchise history with 1,880 total?

   a. Ernie Banks
   b. Sammy Sosa
   c. Cap Anson
   d. Ryne Sandberg

7. Dusty Baker is the Cubs all-time winningest manager.

   a. True
   b. False

8. Which Cub holds the record for most saves in franchise history with 180?

   a. Bruce Sutter
   b. Lee Smith
   c. Carlos Marmol
   d. Ryan Dempster

9. Who holds the Cubs franchise record for stolen bases with 402?

   a. Frank Chance
   b. Walt Wilmot
   c. Johnny Evers
   d. Fred Pfeffer

10. Who holds the Cubs single-season record for hits with 229?

    a. Starlin Castro
    b. Woody English
    c. Rogers Hornsby
    d. Jigger Statz

11. Who holds the Cubs single-season record for home runs with 66?

    a. Hack Wilson
    b. Andre Dawson
    c. Dave Kingman
    d. Sammy Sosa

12. Bill Buckner hit the most sacrifice flies in Cubs' all-time franchise history.

    a. True
    b. False

13. Which pitcher has the most losses in Cubs franchise history with 158?

    a. Charlie Root
    b. Dick Ellsworth

c. Bill Hutchison

d. Guy Bush

14. Which pitcher threw the most complete games in Cubs franchise history with 317?

    a. Clark Griffith

    b. Fred Goldsmith

    c. Bill Hutchison

    d. Mordecai Brown

15. Who is the most intentionally walked Cub of all time?

    a. Ernie Banks

    b. Sammy Sosa

    c. Anthony Rizzo

    d. Don Kessinger

16. Which Cubs hitter holds the single-season record for strikeouts with 199?

    a. Kyle Schwarber

    b. Kris Bryant

    c. Carlos Peña

    d. Javier Báez

17. Clark Griffith has hit the most batters in Cubs franchise history with 116.

    a. True

    b. False

18. Which player has the most plate appearances all-time in Cubs franchise history with a whopping 10,396?

a. Cap Anson
b. Ernie Banks
c. Ron Santo
d. Phil Cavarretta

19. Which pitcher holds the record for most starts in Cubs franchise history with 347?

    a. Fergie Jenkins
    b. Greg Maddux
    c. Hippo Vaughn
    d. Bob Rush

20. Mordecai Brown threw the most shutouts in Cubs history with 48.

    a. True
    b. False

QUIZ ANSWERS

1. B – 545

2. A – True

3. D – 20 times ✗

4. C – Al Spalding ✗

5. A – Fergie Jenkins ✗

6. C – Cap Anson

7. B – False, Cap Anson

8. B – Lee Smith ✗

9. A – Frank Chance ✗

10. C – Rogers Hornsby

11. D – Sammy Sosa

12. B – False, Ernie Banks ✗

13. C – Bill Hutchison ✗

14. C – Bill Hutchison ✗

15. A – Ernie Banks

16. B – Kris Bryant ✗

17. A – True

18. B – Ernie Banks ✗

19. A – Fergie Jenkins ✗

20. A – True

9/20

DID YOU KNOW?

1. Cap Anson holds the No. 1 spot for both hits and doubles in Cubs franchise history, but Jimmy Ryan holds the spot for the most triples.

2. Bill Madlock and Riggs Stephenson are tied for the best career batting average in Cubs franchise history at an impressive .336. Cap Anson and Ray Grimes are tied for third with career batting averages of .331.

3. Eric Young Sr. holds the Cubs franchise record for stolen base percentage with 80.19% success. Good luck throwing him out.

4. Ernie Banks has the most extra-base hits in Cubs franchise history with 1,009. Second on the list is Billy Williams with 881.

5. Fergie Jenkins gave up the most home runs in Cubs franchise history, but he also holds the franchise record for strikeouts with 2,038.

6. Bill Hutchison threw the most wild pitches in Cubs history with 120.

7. Anthony Rizzo holds the top THREE single-season hit-by-pitch records for the Cubs. He was hit a record 30 times in 2015, 27 times in 2019 and 24 times in 2017.

8. Charlie Root holds the Cubs record for most innings pitched at 3,137.1. Close behind him is Bill Hutchison with 3,022.1.

9. John Clarkson holds the Cubs single-season record for wins with 53 in 1885. Second on the list is Al Spalding with 47 in 1876.

10. Randy Myers holds the Cubs single-season records for saves with 53 in 1993. Second on the list is Rod Beck, who saved 51 games in 1998.

CHAPTER 7:

THE TRADE MARKET

QUIZ TIME!

1. In 2012, the Cubs acquired first baseman, Anthony Rizzo from the _____.

    a. Oakland Athletics
    b. New York Yankees
    c. Los Angeles Dodgers
    d. San Diego Padres

2. On July 5, 2014, the Cubs traded Jeff Samardzija and Jason Hammel to the Oakland A's, in exchange for _____, Billy McKinney and Dan Straily.

    a. Kris Bryant
    b. Javier Báez
    c. Addison Russell
    d. Kyle Schwarber

3. In 2009, the Cubs traded right fielder Milton Bradley to the Seattle Mariners in exchange for which starting pitcher?

a. Ryan Dempster

b. Carlos Silva

c. Jeff Samardzija

d. Carlos Zambrano

4. In 2016, the Cubs acquired pitcher Aroldis Chapman from the New York Yankees. How many players did the Cubs trade to the Yanks in order to get Chapman?

a. 1

b. 3

c. 4

d. 7

5. In 2000, the New York Yankees wanted to trade for Sammy Sosa from the Chicago Cubs, but they felt the Cubs were asking for too much.

a. True

b. False

6. In 2015, the Cubs traded Luis Valbuena and Dan Straily to the Houston Astros in exchange for _____.

a. Dexter Fowler

b. Austin Jackson

c. Quintin Berry

d. Dan Haren

7. In 2012, the Cubs traded Ryan Dempster to the Texas Rangers in exchange for _____ and Christian Villanueva.

a. Travis Wood

b. Kyle Hendricks

c. Jake Arrieta

d. Pedro Strop

8. Which team traded Mordecai "Three-Finger" Brown to the Cubs in 1903?

   a. St. Louis Cardinals

   b. New York Highlanders

   c. Boston Americans

   d. Philadelphia Athletics

9. In 1992, the Cubs acquired Sammy Sosa from which MLB team?

   a. Florida Marlins

   b. Detroit Tigers

   c. Minnesota Twins

   d. Chicago White Sox

10. Since the modern, 30-team era began in 1998, the Cubs and St. Louis Cardinals have only made two trades. It currently has been 13 years since their last trade.

    a. True

    b. False

11. Since the 30-team era began in 1998, how many trades have the Cubs made with the Chicago White Sox?

    a. 0 trades

    b. 7 trades

    c. 15 trades

    d. 3 trades

12. The Cubs have currently only made 5 trades with the Tampa Bay Rays ever.

   a. True

   b. False

13. In 1966, the Cubs acquired Hall of Famer Fergie Jenkins from which MLB team?

   a. Philadelphia Phillies
   b. Cincinnati Reds
   c. California Angels
   d. Pittsburgh Pirates

14. The Cubs have never made a trade with the Washington Nationals.

   a. True
   b. False

15. In 2012, Sammy Sosa came out of retirement and signed with the Cubs for one last season to redeem himself after his steroid scandal.

   a. True
   b. False

16. On July 31, 2006, the Chicago Cubs traded _____ to the Los Angeles Dodgers and received Cesar Izturis in return.

   a. Juan Pierre
   b. Carlos Zambrano
   c. Henry Blanco
   d. Greg Maddux

17. In 2013, the Cubs received Jake Arrieta and Pedro Strop from the _____.

    a. Kansas City Royals
    b. Colorado Rockies
    c. Baltimore Orioles
    d. Texas Rangers

18. The Cubs acquired Hall of Famer Ryne Sandberg from which MLB team in 1982?

    a. Atlanta Braves
    b. Philadelphia Phillies
    c. Toronto Blue Jays
    d. Houston Astros

19. The Chicago Cubs have made ___ trades with the Colorado Rockies in franchise history.

    a. 0
    b. 5
    c. 15
    d. 24

20. The Cubs acquired Bill Mueller from the San Francisco Giants in 2000, only to trade him back to the Giants in 2002.

    a. True
    b. False

QUIZ ANSWERS

1. D – San Diego Padres
2. C – Addison Russell
3. B – Carlos Silva
4. C – 4
5. A – True
6. A – Dexter Fowler
7. B – Kyle Hendricks
8. A – St. Louis Cardinals
9. D – Chicago White Sox
10. A – True
11. D – 3 trades
12. A – True
13. A – Philadelphia Phillies
14. B – False
15. B – False
16. D – Greg Maddux
17. C – Baltimore Orioles
18. B – Philadelphia Phillies
19. C – 15
20. A – True

DID YOU KNOW?

1. The Chicago Cubs had the second-largest opening-day payroll in Major League Baseball in 2019 at more than $208 million. The Boston Red Sox had the largest payroll at more than $213 million.

2. The Cubs have made trades with all 30 current MLB teams.

3. In 2007, the Oakland A's traded Jason Kendall and cash to the Cubs for Jerry Blevins and Rob Bowen. A little over a year later, the Cubs traded with the A's again. The A's sent Chad Gaudin and Rich Harden to the Cubs in exchange for Josh Donaldson, Sean Gallagher, Matt Murton and Eric Patterson.

4. In 2011, the Cubs traded D.J. LaMahieu and Tyler Colvin to the Colorado Rockies for Casey Weathers and Ian Stewart. This is regarded as one of the worst trades the Cubs have made. Losing D.J. LaMahieu is seen by many as a tough loss.

5. Current Cubs General Manager Jed Hoyer has been the team's GM since 2011. He is currently signed with the Cubs through 2021. Hoyer was previously the GM for the San Diego Padres.

6. Current Cubs President Theo Epstein has been with the team since 2011 as well. He has a twin brother and

together they have a charity called "A Foundation to Be Named Later."

7. Steve Swisher used to play catcher for the Cubs in the '70s. His son, Nick Swisher made quite a name for himself in the game of baseball about 30 years later.

8. In 2015, the Cubs traded Starlin Castro to the New York Yankees in exchange for Brendan Ryan and Adam Warren.

9. In 1970, the Cubs purchased Joe Pepitone from the Houston Astros. Pepitone had a very successful start to his career with the New York Yankees.

10. In 1974, the Pittsburgh Pirates purchased Tony LaRussa from the Cubs. LaRussa went on to become one of the best Major League Baseball managers of all time.

CHAPTER 8:

DRAFT DAY

QUIZ TIME!

1. With the ___ overall pick in the first round of the 2013 MLB draft, the Chicago Cubs selected 3B Kris Bryant.

    a. 1st
    b. 2nd
    c. 6th
    d. 10th

2. The Cubs have not had the first overall pick in an MLB draft since 1982.

    a. True
    b. False

3. With the 9th overall pick in the first round of the 2011 MLB draft, the Chicago Cubs selected _____.

    a. Dan Vogelbach
    b. Zeke DeVoss
    c. Albert Almora
    d. Javier Báez

4. Which outfielder was chosen by the Cubs 22nd overall in the 1985 MLB draft?

    a. Dave Martinez
    b. Steve Christmas
    c. Rafael Palmeiro
    d. Brian Dayett

5. In 2001, Mark Prior was drafted 2nd overall by the Chicago Cubs. What college was he drafted out of?

    a. San Diego State University
    b. University of Southern California
    c. Stanford University
    d. Cal State Fullerton

6. The Cubs 2014 first-round draft pick, Kyle Schwarber, was drafted out of high school.

    a. True
    b. False

7. The Cubs very first draft pick in franchise history was RHP Rick James in 1965. He was drafted 6th overall in the first round.

    a. True
    b. False

8. With the ___ overall pick in ____round of the 2007 MLB draft, the Chicago Cubs selected C/3B Josh Donaldson.

    a. 3rd, 1st
    b. 48th, 1st
    c. 36th, 16th
    d. 675th, 27th

9. In the 43rd round of the 2009 MLB draft, the Cubs selected which NFL quarterback?

   a. Russell Wilson
   b. Aaron Rodgers
   c. Colin Kaepernick
   d. Cam Newton

10. Back in 1961, the Cubs tried to get famed NFL legend Joe Namath to play for them.

   a. True
   b. False

11. In the first round of the 2020 MLB Draft, the Chicago Cubs selected _____ 16th overall.

   a. Ed Howard
   b. Burl Carraway
   c. Jordan Nwogu
   d. Luke Little

12. The Cubs drafted Anthony Rizzo in the 6th round of the 2007 MLB draft out of Marjory Stoneman Douglas High School.

   a. True
   b. False

13. With the 13th overall pick in the first round of the 2006 MLB draft, the Chicago Cubs selected _____ out of Clemson University. He ended up only playing 6 seasons in the MLB.

   a. Jim Edmonds
   b. Sam Fuld

c. Geovany Soto

d. Tyler Colvin

14. In the 1st round of the 2008 MLB draft, with the 19th overall pick, the Chicago Cubs selected pitcher _____.

a. Andrew Cashner

b. Carlos Marmol

c. Carlos Silva

d. Jeff Gray

15. In the ____ round of the 1984 MLB draft, the Chicago Cubs selected pitcher Greg Maddux.

a. 2nd

b. 1st

c. 12th

d. 21st

16. In 2010, the Cubs selected _____ 6th overall in the first round of the MLB draft. Many regard this as the worst Cubs draft pick of the 2010s. He left the game professionally only three years later.

a. Reggie Golden

b. Micah Gibbs

c. Hunter Ackerman

d. Hayden Simpson

17. With the 6th overall pick in the first round of the 2012 MLB draft, the Chicago Cubs selected _____.

a. Pierce Johnson

b. Stephen Bruno

c. Albert Almora

d. Josh Conway

18. Who did the Cubs draft in the third round with the 67th overall pick of the 1970 MLB draft?

    a. Jeff Wehmeier

    b. Rick Reuschel

    c. Gene Hiser

    d. Roger Metzger

19. With the ____ overall pick of the 1975 MLB draft, the Chicago Cubs selected P Lee Smith in the second round.

    a. 30th

    b. 35th

    c. 40th

    d. 28th

20. In the 2012 MLB draft, the Cubs drafted a whopping 15 high-schoolers.

    a. True

    b. False

QUIZ ANSWERS

1. B – 2nd

2. A – True

3. D – Javier Báez

4. C – Rafael Palmeiro

5. B – University of Southern California

6. B – False

7. A – True

8. B – 48th, 1st

9. C – Colin Kaepernick

10. A – True

11. A – Ed Howard

12. B – False, Boston Red Sox

13. D – Tyler Colvin

14. A – Andrew Cashner

15. A – 2nd

16. D – Hayden Simpson

17. C – Albert Almora

18. B – Rick Reuschel

19. D – 28th

20. A – True

DID YOU KNOW?

1. The Cubs drafted Mark Langston in 1978 in the 15th round. He decided instead to attend San Jose State University. He was later drafted by the Seattle Mariners in the second round of the 1981 MLB draft.

2. The Cubs drafted Mark Grace in the 24th round of the 1985 MLB draft out of San Diego State University. Rafael Palmeiro was drafted by the Cubs the same year. Grace was ultimately chosen over Palmeiro as the Cubs everyday first baseman.

3. Geovany Soto won the 2008 National League Rookie of the Year. He was drafted by the Cubs in the 11th round of the 2001 MLB draft out of the American Military Academy in Puerto Rico.

4. In the 2019 MLB draft, the Chicago Cubs drafted RHP Ryan Jensen 27th overall in the first round out of Fresno State University.

5. Jamie Moyer was drafted by the Chicago Cubs in the 6th round of the 1984 MLB draft out of St. Joseph's University. Moyer went on to play 25 seasons in the MLB. He played until he was 49 years old in 2012.

6. Jeff Samardzija was drafted by the Chicago Cubs in the 5th round of the 2006 MLB draft out of the University of Notre Dame. He was a star football player at Notre Dame

and was recognized as a two-time All-American wide receiver.

7. Kerry Wood was drafted by the Chicago Cubs in the 1st round of the 1995 MLB draft out of Grand Prairie High School. He played 14 seasons of Major League Baseball.

8. The Chicago Cubs drafted IF Ryan Theriot in the 3rd round of the 2001 MLB draft out of Louisiana State University. He played 8 years in the MLB with the Cubs, Dodgers, Cardinals and Giants.

9. Tim Lincecum was drafted by the Cubs in the 48th round of the 2003 MLB draft, but he ultimately did not sign with them so he could attend college. He was drafted two more times – by the Cleveland Indians in the 42nd round in 2005, and then the San Francisco Giants drafted him in the first round with the 10th overall pick in 2006.

10. Pitcher Ken Holtzman was drafted by the Chicago Cubs in the 4th round of the 1965 draft (the first year MLB had a draft) out of the University of Illinois. He ended up playing 15 seasons in the MLB with the Cubs, A's, Orioles and Yankees, then came back full circle to finish his career with the Cubs in 1978 and 1979.

CHAPTER 9:

ODDS & ENDS

QUIZ TIME!

1. Current Cub Anthony Rizzo likes to entertain his teammates by playing _____ by _____ on the electric piano.

   a. *Story of My Life,* One Direction
   b. *Bye Bye Bye,* 'Nsync
   c. *thank u, next,* Ariana Grande
   d. *Hello,* Adele

2. Cubs legend Fergie Jenkins also played basketball for the Harlem Globetrotters.

   a. True
   b. False

3. Which Cub injured his back while sneezing?

   a. Kris Bryant
   b. Jeff Samardzija
   c. Sammy Sosa
   d. Ryne Sandberg

4. Kerry Woods injured his chest when he slipped while
_____.

   a. Chasing his son at the park
   b. Getting out of a hot tub
   c. Washing his car
   d. Watering his vegetable garden

5. Kris Bryant and Jake Arrieta made an appearance in the
Season 5 finale of which popular television show?

   a. Chicago Fire
   b. Modern Family
   c. The Flash
   d. NCIS

6. What tattoo does Javier Báez have on the back of his neck?

   a. A Baseball
   b. The Cubs Logo
   c. The MLB Logo
   d. The Puerto Rican Flag

7. Anthony Rizzo was diagnosed with Hodgkin's Lymphoma
in 2008 and went into remission that same year.

   a. True
   b. False

8. David Ross was the first MLB contestant on which show?

   a. Celebrity MasterChef
   b. Celebrity Big Brother
   c. RuPaul's Celebrity Drag Race
   d. Dancing with the Stars

9. Ryne Sandberg was originally going to play _____ at Washington State University but reversed his commitment when he was drafted into the MLB.

    a. Basketball
    b. Football
    c. Soccer
    d. Lacrosse

10. What kind of animal did Joe Maddon have brought to spring training in 2016 to lighten up the clubhouse atmosphere for his players?

    a. Bear cubs
    b. Cats
    c. Monkeys
    d. Lemurs

11. Which baseball legend is Kyle Schwarber's role model?

    a. Derek Jeter
    b. Rickey Henderson
    c. Johnny Bench
    d. Ken Griffey Jr.

12. Ernie Banks was the first African American player to play for the Cubs in the franchise's history. Gene Baker was the first African American player to sign with the franchise.

    a. True
    b. False

13. After the Cubs won the 2016 World Series, three players made a guest appearance on Saturday Night Live (SNL)

with Bill Murray. Which player below was NOT one of the players who made an appearance?

a. Dexter Fowler
b. Kris Bryant
c. Anthony Rizzo
d. David Ross

14. What hobby does Jake Arrieta work on in his free time?

a. Knitting
b. Gardening
c. Woodworking
d. Building Robots

15. Former Cub Andre Dawson now owns and operates a _____ in Miami, Florida.

a. Irish pub
b. Comic book store
c. Coffee shop
d. Funeral home

16. Dexter Fowler's daughter, Naya, was the flower girl at Anthony Rizzo's wedding.

a. True
b. False

17. Which Cubs pitcher's dad qualified for the PGA Championship in 1991?

a. Cole Hamels
b. Tyler Chatwood

c. Craig Kimbrel

d. Kyle Hendricks

18. In which city does the Cubs Triple-A team play?

    a. Tucson, Arizona

    b. Indianapolis, Indiana

    c. Des Moines, Iowa

    d. Nashville, Tennessee

19. Which Cub is on the cover of the video game, MLB: The Show 20?

    a. Anthony Rizzo

    b. Javier Báez

    c. Kris Bryant

    d. Kyle Schwarber

20. Kris Bryant and Bryce Harper once got thrown out of the MGM Grand in Las Vegas, because security did not believe they were professional baseball players.

    a. True

    b. False

QUIZ ANSWERS

1. D – *Hello,* Adele

2. A – True

3. C – Sammy Sosa

4. B – Getting out of a hot tub

5. A – Chicago Fire

6. C – The MLB Logo

7. A – True

8. D – Dancing with the Stars

9. B – Football

10. A – Bear Cubs

11. C – Johnny Bench

12. A – True

13. B – Kris Bryant

14. C – Woodworking

15. D – Funeral Home

16. A – True

17. D – Kyle Hendricks

18. C – Des Moines, Iowa

19. B – Javier Báez

20. B – False

DID YOU KNOW?

1. Cubs pitcher Yu Darvish can guess someone's blood type by simply engaging in a conversation with them and getting to know their personality.

2. Cubs catcher Wilson Contreras has a brother named William who plays in the Atlanta Braves' organization. During the COVID-19 pandemic, they both took batting practice with each other in Wilson's driveway to stay in shape.

3. Cubs third baseman Kris Bryant married his high school sweetheart, Jessica. They even had their engagement pictures taken at Wrigley Field.

4. Kris Bryant's dad, Mike, played in the New York Mets' organization in the '80s. Although he never made it to the big leagues like his son, it just shows the game runs through the blood of the Bryants.

5. Cubs outfielder Ian Happ considers himself a coffee connoisseur. During the COVID-19 pandemic, he teamed up with a brewing company to sell "Quarantine Coffee," whose profits were donated to charity benefitting COVID-19 relief efforts.

6. Anthony Rizzo and Jason Heyward were born exactly one day apart. Rizzo was born on August 8, 1989 and Heyward was born on August 9, 1989.

7. Pitcher Derek Holland was once kicked out of a Counting Crows concert in New Jersey while visiting to play the New York Yankees.

8. Former Cubs manager Joe Maddon has a serious passion for cycling. He says he bikes anywhere from 60-100 miles per week. He loves staying in shape and the mental benefits that cycling provides him.

9. The first Cubs manager, Al Spalding, had a nephew, also named Albert, who became a famous concert violinist.

10. In high school, Kyle Schwarber was an athlete who played football and, of course, baseball, but he also took part in show choir. Seriously ... look it up on YouTube. The Cubs even had Schwarber and fellow teammates re-enact a performance back in 2016.

CHAPTER 10:

OUTFIELDERS

QUIZ TIME!

1. Which team did former Cubs outfielder Andre Dawson NOT play for during his career?

   a. Montreal Expos
   b. Boston Red Sox
   c. Detroit Tigers
   d. Florida Marlins

2. Former Cubs outfielder Milton Bradley has no relation whatsoever to the board game company of the same name.

   a. True
   b. False

3. In what year was former Cub Billy Williams elected to the National Baseball Hall of Fame?

   a. 1987
   b. 1995
   c. 1993
   d. 1983

4. Former Cub outfielder David DeJesus never hit a home run in his two years spent on the team.

    a. True
    b. False

5. Which of these teams has former MLB outfielder and former Cubs manager Dusty Baker NOT managed (so far at least) in his coaching career?

    a. San Francisco Giants
    b. Washington Nationals
    c. Cincinnati Reds
    d. Texas Rangers

6. How many games did outfielder Quintin Berry play in his 2015 season with the Cubs?

    a. 80
    b. 8
    c. 18
    d. 128

7. Hank Sauer played his entire 15-year career with the Cubs.

    a. True
    b. False

8. How many seasons did Phil Cavarretta play for the Cubs?

    a. 5
    b. 12
    c. 20
    d. He was never a Cub

9. How many World Series did former Cub Matt Stairs win during his 19-year MLB career?

    a. 4
    b. 9
    c. 1
    d. 3

10. David DeJesus' wife, Kim, was a contestant on which popular TV show?

    a. Big Brother
    b. The Amazing Race
    c. The Bachelor
    d. Survivor

11. Which former MLB outfielder and former Cubs manager is one of only two players in the MLB to reach the World Series in three consecutive years with three different teams?

    a. Dusty Baker
    b. Joe Altobelli
    c. Don Baylor
    d. Lou Piniella

12. Cole Gillespie played a combined 206 games in 5 seasons, all with the Cubs.

    a. True
    b. False

13. How many home runs did OF Kyle Schwarber hit as a member of the Cubs during the 2019 season?

a. 38

b. 30

c. 26

d. 16

14. What place did OF Ian Happ come in for the 2017 National League Rookie of the Year voting?

    a. 1st

    b. 4th

    c. 6th

    d. 8th

15. What was OF Albert Almora's season batting average in 2017?

    a. .277

    b. .298

    c. .286

    d. .236

16. Jason Heyward hit only one triple in his first season with the Cubs.

    a. True

    b. False

17. How many games did Dexter Fowler appear in for the Cubs during the 2015 season?

    a. 12

    b. 44

    c. 139

    d. 156

18. Former Cub Ralph Kiner ranked 4 seasons in the top ten of which stat?

    a. WAR

    b. Stolen bases

    c. At-bat's

    d. Hit by pitch

19. Which player came in 2nd for most NL outfield assists during the 2018 season?

    a. Ian Happ

    b. Kyle Schwarber

    c. Albert Almora

    d. Jason Heyward

20. Ian Happ was named the National League Player of the Week on September 29, 2019.

    a. True

    b. False

QUIZ ANSWERS

1. C – Detroit Tigers ✗
2. A – True
3. A – 1987 ✗
4. B – False, he hit 9 in 2012, 6 in 2013 ✗
5. D – Texas Rangers ✗
6. B – 8 ✗
7. B – False ✗
8. C – 20 ✗
9. C – 1
10. B – The Amazing Race ✗
11. C – Don Baylor ✗
12. B – False, Gene Hiser ✗
13. A – 38 ✗
14. D – 8th ✗
15. B –.298 ✗
16. A – True
17. D – 156 ✗
18. A – WAR ✓
19. B – Kyle Schwarber ✗
20. A – True

4/20

DID YOU KNOW?

1. Former Cubs outfielder Chuck Klein was the first left-handed hitter in the National League to win the Triple Crown. A player wins the Triple Crown by leading one of the major leagues in home runs, RBI and batting average for a season.

2. Former Cubs outfielder Dexter Fowler represented the United States in the 2008 Summer Olympics as a member of the national baseball team.

3. Before Andre Dawson became known as "The Hawk," a nickname his uncle gave him, his family referenced to him as "Pudgy."

4. Former Cubs outfielder Nate Schierholtz is now an operating partner for KLV Capital and he has an Arizona real estate license.

5. Former Cubs outfielder Doug Glanville has been an MLB analyst at ESPN for over 10 years. He is also a professor at the University of Connecticut.

6. Former Cubs outfielder Derrick May was a hitting coach for the St. Louis Cardinals and their minor league teams after his playing career ended. He also was a hitting coach in the Colorado Rockies' organization for one season in 2017.

7. Former Cubs outfielder Matt Stairs was a hitting coach for the Philadelphia Phillies and San Diego Padres after his playing career ended.

8. In 2016, current Cubs outfielder Kyle Schwarber became the first position player in MLB history to get his first hit of the season during the World Series.

9. Current Cubs outfielder Ian Happ was the fastest player in Cubs franchise history to reach 20 home runs in his career. He did so in just 89 games.

10. Cubs outfielder Jason Heyward was the second-youngest player ever to hit a home run in his first major league at-bat when he did so in 2010.

CHAPTER 11:

INFIELDERS

QUIZ TIME!

1. Which former Cubs infielder hit a home run in his first MLB at-bat and drove in 6 runs in that same game?

    a. Aramis Ramírez
    b. Darwin Barney
    c. Anthony Rizzo
    d. Starlin Castro

2. "Mr. Cub," Ernie Banks, served in the United States Army during the Korean War.

    a. True
    b. False

3. After retirement, which former Cubs infielder took a position as a studio analyst for the MLB Network and became the broadcast announcer in the video game, MLB: The Show?

    a. Nomar Garciaparra
    b. Ben Zobrist

c. Mark DeRosa

d. Ryan Theriot

4. How many games did Anthony Rizzo play in for the Cubs in 2015?

   a. 120
   b. 150
   c. 160
   d. 100

5. Former Cubs infielder Nomar Garciaparra is married to which soccer star?

   a. Alex Morgan
   b. Mia Hamm
   c. Hope Solo
   d. Lindsey Horan

6. "Mr. Cub," Ernie Banks received the Presidential Medal of Freedom from which former U.S. president?

   a. John F. Kennedy
   b. Richard Nixon
   c. Bill Clinton
   d. Barack Obama

7. Ron Santo was named to 10 MLB All-Star Games.

   a. True
   b. False

8. Which former Cubs infielder came in 1st with the most triples during the 1984 season in the National League with 19?

a. Ryne Sandberg

b. Bill Buckner

c. Larry Bowa

d. Dave Owen

9. Former Cubs infielder Billy Williams only played for two MLB teams during his 18-season career. Which team other than the Cubs did he play for?

a. Baltimore Orioles

b. Oakland A's

c. Minnesota Twins

d. Chicago White Sox

10. How many home runs did Ernie Banks hit in his 19 seasons with Chicago?

a. 525

b. 501

c. 512

d. 499

11. How many home runs did Kris Bryant hit in the 2016 season?

a. 26

b. 29

c. 31

d. 39

12. Former Cubs infielder Starlin Castro was the first MLB player who was born in the 1990s.

a. True

b. False

13. Which former Cubs infielder came in first in outs made in the National League in 1968 with 526?

    a. Ron Santo
    b. Ernie Banks
    c. Don Kessinger
    d. Vic LaRose

14. Which university did the Cubs draft 1B Mark Grace from in 1985?

    a. San Diego State University
    b. University of North Carolina at Chapel Hill
    c. Vanderbilt University
    d. UC Davis

15. What uniform number did Ernie Banks wear for his entire career with the Cubs?

    a. No. 44
    b. No. 31
    c. No. 14
    d. No. 2

16. Javier Báez has never been named to an MLB All-Star Game.

    a. True
    b. False

17. There are three statues erected outside of Wrigley Field. One is of Harry Caray, the other two are of former Cubs infielders. Which infielders are they?

    a. Anthony Rizzo and Kris Bryant
    b. Ron Santo and Ryne Sandberg

c. Ernie Banks and Ryne Sandberg

d. Ernie Banks and Ron Santo

18. Which Cubs infielder was named the 2016 NLCS MVP?

a. Javier Báez

b. Anthony Rizzo

c. Kris Bryant

d. Tommy La Stella

19. Former Cubs infielder Ryne Sandberg spent all but one season of his 16-year MLB career with the Cubs. What other MLB team did Sandberg play for and get drafted by?

a. Kansas City Royals

b. New York Mets

c. Los Angeles Dodgers

d. Philadelphia Phillies

20. Cubs third baseman Kris Bryant currently wears No. 44.

a. True

b. False

QUIZ ANSWERS

1. D – Starlin Castro

2. A – True

3. C – Mark DeRosa

4. C – 160

5. B – Mia Hamm

6. D – Barack Obama

7. B – False, 9

8. A – Ryne Sandberg

9. B – Oakland A's

10. C – 512

11. D – 39

12. A – True

13. C – Don Kessinger

14. A – San Diego State University

15. C – No. 14

16. B – False, 2 (so far)

17. D – Ernie Banks and Ron Santo

18. A – Javier Báez

19. D – Philadelphia Phillies

20. B – False, No. 17

DID YOU KNOW?

1. Former Cubs infielder and manager Don Zimmer played for the Brooklyn Dodgers, Los Angeles Dodgers, New York Mets, Cincinnati Reds, Washington Senators and, of course, the Cubs in his 12-year MLB playing career. He managed the San Diego Padres, Boston Red Sox, Texas Rangers and the Cubs in his 13-year MLB managerial career.

2. Ernie Banks is one of only 13 players in MLB history to win consecutive MVP Awards.

3. Third baseman Stan Hack played 16 seasons from 1932-1947, all with the Cubs. He hit 57 home runs in his career and had 2,193 hits in 7,278 at-bats.

4. Harry Steinfeldt won two World Series with the Cubs. Not many players can say this. He played for the Cubs from 1906 through 1910.

5. Anthony Rizzo leads all Cubs first basemen in franchise history in home runs with 217 as of the end of the 2019 season.

6. Mark Grace hit 456 doubles when he was with the Cubs, which is second in franchise history.

7. Frank Chance has the most stolen bases in Cubs franchise history with 402.

8. Cap Anson has the highest WAR (Wins Above Replacement) in Cubs franchise history with a whopping 84.8.

9. Bill Buckner is usually remembered for his mishap with the Red Sox, but his time with the Cubs should be remembered as well. With the Cubbies, he hit .300 with 1,136 hits in 7 seasons.

10. Glenn Beckert led the MLB in runs in 1968 with 98.

CHAPTER 12:

PITCHERS AND CATCHERS

QUIZ TIME!

1. How many MLB teams did David Ross play for in his 15-year MLB career?

    a. 2
    b. 5
    c. 7
    d. 12

2. In 2016, David Ross became the oldest player to hit a home run in Game 7 of the World Series.

    a. True
    b. False

3. Which former Cubs pitcher threw a no-hitter on August 19, 1969, without recording any strikeouts?

    a. Fergie Jenkins
    b. Ken Holtzman
    c. Ted Abernathy
    d. Joe Niekro

4. Which former Cubs manager was never a catcher in his playing career?

   a. Silver Flint
   b. Bruce Kimm
   c. Dale Sveum
   d. El Tappe

5. Lee Smith spent 8 seasons with the Cubs but played 10 more seasons in his career after that. Which of the teams below did Smith NOT play for?

   a. Montreal Expos
   b. California Angels
   c. Boston Red Sox
   d. Houston Astros

6. Which former Cubs pitcher holds the record for fastest pitch ever thrown, at 105.1 mph?

   a. Greg Maddux
   b. Aroldis Chapman
   c. Fergie Jenkins
   d. Kerry Wood

7. Fergie Jenkins was named to 3 MLB All-Star Games in his career.

   a. True
   b. False

8. Which former Cubs pitcher threw the most strikeouts in the National League in 2003 with 266?

   a. Carlos Zambrano
   b. Kerry Wood

c. Mark Prior

d. Kyle Farnsworth

9. Which Cubs catcher caught the most runners stealing in the National League in 2018 with 27?

   a. Chris Gimenez

   b. Miguel Montero

   c. Willson Contreras

   d. Alex Avila

10. Which Cubs pitcher had the most wins in the National League in 2015 with 22?

   a. Jake Arrieta

   b. Jon Lester

   c. Jason Hammel

   d. Kyle Hendricks

11. Which MLB team did former Cubs catcher Geovany Soto NOT play for during his career?

   a. Oakland A's

   b. Los Angeles Angels of Anaheim

   c. New York Yankees

   d. Chicago White Sox

12. John Lackey was only 19 when he made his MLB debut.

   a. True

   b. False

13. What uniform number did Carlos Zambrano wear during his career with the Cubs?

a. No. 46

b. No. 77

c. No. 11

d. No. 38

14. How many MLB All-Star Games was Hall of Famer Greg Maddux named to in his 23-season career?

    a. 0

    b. 4

    c. 8

    d. 15

15. Before former catcher David Ross was named the Cubs manager, what role did he play for the Cubs after he retired as a player?

    a. Front office special assistant

    b. Hitting coach

    c. Bench coach

    d. Director of player personnel

16. Mordecai "Three-Finger" Brown only pitched for the Cubs for two seasons.

    a. True

    b. False

17. What year was the first perfect game in Cubs history thrown?

    a. 1995

    b. 2006

    c. 2016

    d. No Cubs pitcher has ever thrown a perfect game

18. How many intentional walks did former Cubs pitcher Rick Sutcliffe throw during the 1990 season?

    a. 0
    b. 2
    c. (4)
    d. 5

19. How many saves did Bruce Sutter record for the Cubs during the 1979 season?

    a. 10
    b. 45
    c. 26
    d. 37

20. Former Cubs pitcher Randy Myers is the cousin of comedian and actor Mike Myers.

    a. True
    b. False

QUIZ ANSWERS

1. C- 7

2. A – True

3. B – Ken Holtzman

4. C – Dale Sveum ✗

5. D – Houston Astros ✗

6. B – Aroldis Chapman

7. A – True

9/20

8. B – Kerry Wood ✗

9. C – Willson Contreras

10. A – Jake Arrieta ✗

11. C – New York Yankees ✗

12. B – False, 23 ✗

13. D – No. 38

14. C – 8

15. A – Front office special assistant ✗

16. B – False, 10 ✗

17. D – No Cubs pitcher has ever thrown a perfect game

18. A – 0 ✗

19. D – 37 ✗

20. B – False ✗

DID YOU KNOW?

1. Of the six pitchers in MLB history who have thrown at least three no-hitters, former Cubs legend Larry Corcoran is the only one who is retired and not in the National Baseball Hall of Fame. He was also able to pitch with both arms.

2. Joe Girardi may be known to many today as the former manager of the Yankees. During his playing career, he was a catcher for the Cubs from 1989 to 1992 and again from 2000 to 2002.

3. Former Cubs catcher Henry Blanco spent three seasons in the top 10 list of assists by a catcher.

4. Fergie Jenkins made a whopping SEVEN Opening Day starts for the Cubs during his career.

5. After retirement, former Cubs catcher Jason Kendall wrote a book called "Throwback". David Ross also wrote a book after his retirement called "Teammate."

6. Former Cubs pitcher Ryan Dempster is the only pitcher in Cubs franchise history with at least 50 saves and at least 50 wins with the team.

7. Lee Smith had 11 seasons with 30 or more saves. His career save percentage was 82%.

8. On May 6, 1998, Kerry Wood threw a 20-strikeout game at only 20 years old. It was a complete game for Wood and he only allowed one hit.

9. Sons of Kent Brewery released a limited-edition beer in 2019 to honor former Cubs pitcher Fergie Jenkins called

Fergie's Classic Pilsner. Proceeds were donated to a treatment center for children. Fergie was the first Canadian MLB player to be elected to the Hall of Fame.

10. Greg Maddux did not attend college, he was drafted out of high school in 1984.

CHAPTER 13:

108 YEARS

QUIZ TIME!

1. How many World Series have the Cubs won?

   a. 1
   b. 3
   c. 6
   d. 9

2. The Cubs went 108 years without winning a World Series, an MLB record.

   a. True
   b. False

3. Which player was named World Series MVP in 2016?

   a. Anthony Rizzo
   b. Kris Bryant
   c. Javier Báez
   d. Ben Zobrist

4. Before the Cubs won the World Series in 2016, their only other two World Championships came in ____ and _____.

    a. 1914 and 1919
    b. 1908 and 1910
    c. 1907 and 1908
    d. 1901 and 1902

5. What is the name of the fan who "cursed" the Cubs in the 2003 postseason by catching a fly ball that the leftfielder was trying to catch?

    a. Steve Bartman
    b. Steve Goatman
    c. Bart Stevensen
    d. Bart Stevens

6. How many games did the 2016 World Series go?

    a. 3
    b. 5
    c. 6
    d. 7

7. The Cubs had a "curse" put on them, called "The Curse of the Billy Goat" by a tavern owner in 1945.

    a. True
    b. False

8. Who was the Cubs manager when they won the World Series in 2016?

    a. Lou Piniella
    b. Rick Renteria

c. Joe Maddon
d. Dusty Baker

9. Who was the Cubs manager during both the 1907 and the 1908 World Series wins?

   a. Cap Anson
   b. Al Spalding
   c. Frank Chance
   d. Johnny Evers

10. Who did the Cubs defeat in the 2016 World Series?

    a. Detroit Tigers
    b. Cleveland Indians
    c. Houston Astros
    d. Texas Rangers

11. Who did the Cubs defeat in the 1907 AND 1908 World Series?

    a. Detroit Tigers
    b. New York Yankees
    c. Boston Red Sox
    d. Washington Senators

12. The 2016 World Series featured the two teams with the longest World Series win droughts in the MLB with a combined 176 years between them.

    a. True
    b. False

13. While entering the 10th inning of Game 7 of the 2016 World Series, what interrupted the game and resulted in a 17-minute delay?

   a. A fan ran across the field
   b. Rain
   c. The lights went out
   d. An umpire was injured and had to be replaced

14. Which Cubs player was the first player in MLB history to hit a leadoff home run in a Game 7 of the World Series?

   a. Javier Báez
   b. Kris Bryant
   c. Anthony Rizzo
   d. Dexter Fowler

15. Which 2016 Cub became a back-to-back World Series champion in 2016 after playing for the Kansas City Royals the previous season?

   a. Jason Heyward
   b. Trevor Cahill
   c. Ben Zobrist
   d. Munenori Kawasaki

16. The Cubs 2016 World Series rings are worth about $70,000 each and consist of 5.5 carats of diamonds, 3 carats of rubies and 2.5 carats of sapphires.

   a. True
   b. False

17. Who was the Cubs starting pitcher for Game 7 of the 2016 World Series?

    a. Jon Lester

    b. Kyle Hendricks

    c. Jake Arrieta

    d. Jason Hammel

18. What was the final score of Game 7 of the 2016 World Series?

    a. 8-7

    b. 9-7

    c. 10-9

    d. 9-8

19. Which Cub did NOT hit a home run in Game 7 of the 2016 World Series?

    a. Dexter Fowler

    b. Kyle Schwarber

    c. Javier Báez

    d. David Ross

20. David Ross ended his playing career with a home run in Game 7 of the World Series.

    a. True

    b. False

QUIZ ANSWERS

1. B – 3

2. A – True

3. D – Ben Zobrist

4. C – 1907 and 1908 ✗

5. A – Steve Bartman

6. D – 7

7. A – True

8. C – Joe Maddon

9. C – Frank Chance ✗

10. B – Cleveland Indians

11. A – Detroit Tigers ✗

12. A – True

13. B – Rain ✗

14. D – Dexter Fowler

15. C – Ben Zobrist

16. A – True ✗

17. B – Kyle Hendricks ✗

18. A – 8-7 ✗

19. B – Kyle Schwarber

20. A – True

13/20

DID YOU KNOW?

1. In the final game of the 1908 World Series against the Tigers, there were only 6,210 spectators in attendance and the game lasted only 1 hour and 25 minutes. The final game of the 2016 World Series had 38,104 in attendance and lasted 4 hours and 28 minutes.

2. "Mr. Cub," Ernie Banks, played his entire 19-season career with the Cubs and never even got to the playoffs, let alone win a World Series championship. He holds the MLB record for most games played without a playoff appearance.

3. The movies, "Taking Care of Business" and "Back to the Future Part II" both mention the Cubs winning the World Series. Both of those films are 108 minutes long. The Cubs were in a World Series drought for 108 years.

4. Before 2016, the last time the Cubs had won a World Series game was on October 8, 1945. The Cubs were in a World Series drought for 108 years after that.

5. The Cubs won the 1907 World Series in a 4-game sweep over the Tigers but played 5 games total. Game One resulted in a 3-3 tie after 12 innings.

6. The Cubs won the 1908 World Series, allowing the Tigers to win only one game and taking the Series 4-1.

7. Mordecai "Three-Finger" Brown earned the win in relief

after blowing the save Game 1 of the 1908 World Series for the Cubs.

8. Anthony Rizzo played in all 7 games of the 2016 World Series. In 25 at-bats, he hit 1 home run, drove in 5 runs, scored 7 runs and got 9 hits.

9. Kris Bryant played in all 7 games of the 2016 World Series. In 26 at-bats, he hit 2 home runs, knocked in 2 runs, scored 6 runs and got 7 hits.

10. Javier Báez played in all 7 games of the 2016 World Series. In 30 at-bats, he had five hits, including a home run that was his only RBI and only run scored in the series.

CHAPTER 14:

HEATED RIVALRIES

QUIZ TIME!

1. How many times have the Cubs and White Sox played each other in the World Series?

    a. 0 times
    b. 1 time
    c. 11 times
    d. 12 times

2. The Cubs-Cardinals rivalry is often referred to as the Route 66 Rivalry and the I-55 Rivalry.

    a. True
    b. False

3. The Cubs and St. Louis Cardinals have met once in the MLB Playoffs. The Cubs won three games to one. What year did this NLDS matchup occur?

    a. 1995
    b. 2004
    c. 2012
    d. 2015

4. In June 2020, the Cubs and Cardinals were supposed to play a series in _____ but the series was canceled due to the COVID-19 pandemic.

    a. Paris, France
    b. Barcelona, Spain
    c. London, England
    d. Dublin, Ireland

5. Which Cub and Cardinal had a 1998 rivalry chasing the MLB home run record?

    a. Sammy Sosa & J.D. Drew
    b. Sammy Sosa & Mark McGwire
    c. Mark Grace & Mark McGwire
    d. Mark Grace & Delino DeShields

6. The Cubs have three World Championships as of the 2019 season. How many do the Cardinals have?

    a. 11
    b. 13
    c. 6
    d. 4

7. The Cubs and Cardinals shared Wrigley Field for a short period of time, which was a big part of their rivalry.

    a. True
    b. False

8. On May 15, 1960, which pitcher threw a no-hitter against the St. Louis Cardinals in his Cubs debut?

    a. Bob Anderson

b. Moe Drabowsky

c. John Goetz

d. Don Cardwell

9. What nickname is NOT used to describe a series between the Cubs and the Chicago White Sox?

a. Crosstown Classic

b. The Windy City Showdown

c. CubSox Showdown

d. North-South Showdown

10. How many games did the 1906 World Series between the Cubs and White Sox go?

a. 4

b. 5

c. 6

d. 7

11. The Cubs-White Sox rivalry became physical when a brawl broke out on May 20, 2006, between which players?

a. Ryan Dempster and Sandy Alomar Jr.

b. Ryan Dempster and Jermaine Dye

c. Greg Maddux and A.J. Pierzynski

d. Michael Barrett and A.J. Pierzynski

12. Rick Renteria has been a manager for both the Cubs and the White Sox.

a. True

b. False

13. Which former White Sox manager once said, "But one thing about Wrigley Field, I puke every time I go there"?

 a. Robin Ventura
 b. Ozzie Guillén
 c. Gene Lamont
 d. Eddie Stanky

14. Which player has NOT played for both the Cubs and the White Sox?

 a. Ron Santo
 b. Jeff Samardzija
 c. Don Kessinger
 d. Aramis Ramírez

15. Which player has NOT played for both the Cubs and the Cardinals?

 a. Ryan Theriot
 b. Mark Grace
 c. Lee Smith
 d. Lou Brock

16. The Cubs played the White Sox in the first game at Comiskey Park on July 1, 1910.

 a. True
 b. False

17. The Cubs have three World Championships as of the 2019 season. How many do the White Sox have?

 a. 1
 b. 2

c. 3

d. 6

18. Before the 2019 season, which Cub is quoted as saying, "Who would want to play in St. Louis? So boring."

   a. Kris Bryant

   b. Anthony Rizzo

   c. Javier Báez

   d. Kyle Schwarber

19. In 2005, the Cubs Derrek Lee and Cardinals' Albert Pujols were locked in a tight NL MVP Race. Who ended up winning the honor that year?

   a. Lee

   b. Pujols

   c. It was a tie

   d. Neither of them

20. The "Crosstown Cup" was created in 2010 and whoever wins the series between the Cubs and White Sox wins the trophy.

   a. True

   b. False

QUIZ ANSWERS

1. B – 1 time (1906)

2. A – True

3. D – 2015

4. C – London, England

5. B – Sammy Sosa & Mark McGwire

6. A – 11

7. B – False

8. D – Don Cardwell

9. C – CubSox Showdown

10. C – 6

11. D – Michael Barrett and A.J. Pierzynski

12. A – True

13. B – Ozzie Guillén

14. D – Aramis Ramírez

15. B – Mark Grace

16. B – False, St. Louis Browns

17. C – 3

18. A – Kris Bryant

19. B – Pujols

20. A – True

DID YOU KNOW?

1. Ryan Theriot was acquired by the Cardinals in 2010 and was quoted as saying he was "finally on the right side of the Cardinals-Cubs rivalry." It's safe to say many Cubs players were unhappy with his comment.

2. The first meeting between the Cardinals and Cubs as members of the National League took place on April 12, 1892, at Sportsman's Park in St. Louis, MO.

3. The Chicago Transit Authority's Red Line train has stops within a block of both Wrigley Field and Guaranteed Rate Field.

4. The 1906 World Series was the first to feature two teams from the same city.

5. The Cubs Hack Wilson jumped into the stands to attack a heckling Cardinals fan in 1928. Five thousand fans swarmed the field in a riot and the fan sued Wilson for $20,000, but Wilson ultimately won the case.

6. The Cubs/Cardinals rivalry was heightened even more when Dexter Fowler decided to sign with the Cardinals the year after the Cubs won the 2016 World Series championship.

7. The Cubs/Cardinals rivalry is an important geographical stamp in the Netflix show, "Ozark." A couple of direct quotes from the show are: "I was raised to hate the Cubs" and "I was raised to hate the Cardinals."

8. Hall of Famer Rogers Hornsby holds several single-season hitting records for both the Cubs and the Cardinals.

9. The 1906 World Series basically put Chicago as a city on hold for about a week. Again, the two teams have only ever met in the World Series once … so far at least.

10. President Barack Obama is an avid White Sox fan but his wife Michelle is an avid Cubs fan. They both grew up in Chicago.

CHAPTER 15:

THE AWARDS SECTION

QUIZ TIME!

1. Which Cubs pitcher was the first pitcher in MLB history to win the Cy Young Award four seasons in a row?

    a. Greg Maddux
    b. Jon Lester
    c. Fergie Jenkins
    d. Kerry Wood

2. No Cubs manager has ever won the National League Manager of the Year Award.

    a. True
    b. False

3. Who was the first Cubs pitcher to win the Cy Young Award?

    a. Greg Maddux
    b. Bruce Sutter
    c. Fergie Jenkins
    d. Rick Sutcliffe

4. Which Cub most recently won the Rookie of the Year Award?

    a. Javier Báez

    b. Kris Bryant

    c. Geovany Soto

    d. Kerry Wood

5. How many Gold Glove Awards did Ryne Sandberg accumulate during his playing career?

    a. 5

    b. 2

    c. 9

    d. 12

6. Who is the only player in Cubs history to win a Platinum Glove Award?

    a. Ian Happ

    b. Javier Báez

    c. Kris Bryant

    d. Anthony Rizzo

7. No Cubs pitcher has ever won a Silver Slugger Award.

    a. True

    b. False

8. Which two Cubs split the NLCS MVP honor in the 2016 playoffs?

    a. Anthony Rizzo and Kris Bryant

    b. Javier Báez and Jon Lester

    c. Jake Arrieta and Kyle Schwarber

    d. David Ross and Kris Bryant

9. Which Cub has NOT won an MLB Home Run Derby?

   a. Sammy Sosa
   b. Ryne Sandberg
   c. Anthony Rizzo
   d. Andre Dawson

10. What year did Theo Epstein win Sporting News' Executive of the Year Award?

   a. 2019
   b. 2003
   c. 2008
   d. 2016

11. Which Cub won the 1998 NL Rookie of the Year Award?

   a. Sammy Sosa
   b. Kerry Wood
   c. Mark Grace
   d. Terry Mulholland

12. Only one Cubs player has ever won the MLB All-Star Game MVP Award.

   a. True
   b. False

13. Which Cub has NOT won an NL Hank Aaron Award?

   a. Ryne Sandberg
   b. Kris Bryant
   c. Sammy Sosa
   d. Aramis Ramírez

14. What year was Harry Caray named to the NAB Broadcasting Hall of Fame?

    a. 2002
    b. 1994
    c. 1990
    d. 2000

15. Which Cub won the 2016 ESPY Award for Best Breakthrough Athlete?

    a. Javier Báez
    b. Kyle Schwarber
    c. Jake Arrieta
    d. Kris Bryant

16. Anthony Rizzo won the 2016 National League MVP Award.

    a. True
    b. False

17. How many of his 18 career Gold Glove Awards did Greg Maddux win with the Cubs?

    a. 8
    b. 1
    c. 3
    d. 5

18. Which Cub is the only player in franchise history to win the National League MVP Award in back-to-back seasons?

    a. Rogers Hornsby
    b. Sammy Sosa

c. Ryne Sandberg

d. Ernie Banks

19. How many Silver Slugger Awards did Sammy Sosa win in his career?

a. 12

b. 6

c. 3

d. 0

20. Geovany Soto took home the Players Choice Award for National League Outstanding Rookie in 2008.

a. True

b. False

QUIZ ANSWERS

1. A – Greg Maddux

2. B – False: 1984 Jim Frey, 1989 Don Zimmer, 2008 Lou Piniella, 2015 Joe Maddon

3. C – Fergie Jenkins

4. B – Kris Bryant

5. C – 9

6. D – Anthony Rizzo

7. B – False, Carlos Zambrano, Jake Arrieta

8. B – Javier Báez and Jon Lester

9. C – Anthony Rizzo

10. D – 2016

11. B – Kerry Wood

12. A – True, Bill Madlock

13. A – Ryne Sandberg

14. B – 1994

15. C – Jake Arrieta

16. B – False, Kris Bryant

17. D – 5

18. D – Ernie Banks

19. B-6

20. A – True

DID YOU KNOW?

1. The DHL Hometown Heroes Award was a fan-voted award in 2006 given to the best player in franchise history based on leadership, character and baseball talent. "Mr. Cub," Ernie Banks, was chosen for this award for Chicago.

2. The Chicago Cubs were named the Organization of the Year by Baseball America in 2016 after their historic World Series win.

3. Ron Santo won 5 Gold Gloves in five consecutive seasons during his career with the Cubs in 1964, 1965, 1966, 1967 and 1968.

4. Five Cubs have been awarded Cy Young Awards. They are Fergie Jenkins (1971), Bruce Sutter (1979), Rick Sutcliffe (1984), Greg Maddux (1992) and Jake Arrieta (2015).

5. Six Cubs have been named Rookie of the Year: Billy Williams (1961), Ken Hubbs (1962), Jerome Walton (1989), Kerry Wood (1998), Geovany Soto (2008) and Kris Bryant (2015).

6. Ten Cubs players have been named National League MVP in 11 different seasons. Those MVPs are Frank Schulte (1911), Rogers Hornsby (1929), Gabby Hartnett (1935), Phil Cavarretta (1945), Hank Sauer (1952), Ernie Banks (1958 and 1959), Ryne Sandberg (1984), Andre Dawson (1987), Sammy Sosa (1998) and Kris Bryant (2016).

7. Ryne Sandberg holds the record for most Gold Glove Awards won with the Cubs in franchise history with 9. Ron Santo and Greg Maddux each won 5 Gold Gloves in Chicago.

8. Ryne Sandberg currently holds the record for the most Silver Slugger Awards in Cubs history with 7. Sammy Sosa is in second place with 6.

9. Three Cubs have won the NL Hank Aaron Award: Sammy Sosa (1999), Aramis Ramírez (2008) and Kris Bryant (2016).

10. The Cubs have had three Home Run Derby Champions. They are Andre Dawson (1987), Ryne Sandberg (1990) and Sammy Sosa (2000).

CHAPTER 16:

THE WINDY CITY

QUIZ TIME!

1. Which of these treats was created in Chicago?

    a. Zebra Cakes
    b. Twinkies
    c. Sno-Balls
    d. Devil Cremes

2. Chicago is home to the world's first color TV station.

    a. True
    b. False

3. What is unique about the Chicago River?

    a. It is the only river in the world that contains no fish
    b. It is the only river in the world that contains no water
    c. It is the smallest river in the world
    d. It is the only river in the world that flows backward

4. What is the name of the tower where you can view four states at once (Illinois, Wisconsin, Indiana and Michigan)?

    a. Coit Tower
    b. Space Needle
    c. Willis Tower
    d. Eiffel Tower

5. Which was NOT invented in Chicago?

    a. Spray Paint
    b. Nicotine Patch
    c. Vacuum Cleaner
    d. Zipper

6. The Field Museum holds the world's most complete T-Rex skeleton. What is her name?

    a. Lisa
    b. Sophia
    c. Sue
    d. Natasha

7. Route 66 starts in Chicago.

    a. True
    b. False

8. For which holiday does the Plumber's Union dye the Chicago River green?

    a. Christmas
    b. St. Patrick's Day
    c. Earth Day
    d. Halloween

9. What is the name of the park where "The Bean" is on display?

   a. Millennium Park
   b. Lincoln Park
   c. Garfield Park
   d. Jackson Park

10. What year was Chicago founded?

   a. 1803
   b. 1933
   c. 1833
   d. 1830

11. The city of Chicago is home to the world's largest free outdoor food festival. What is the name of that festival?

   a. The Taste of the Windy City
   b. Windy City Food Festival
   c. Illinois Food Festival
   d. The Taste of Chicago

12. Gotham City from the popular comic, *Batman* is based on Chicago.

   a. True
   b. False

13. How much does a ticket to the Lincoln Park Zoo cost?

   a. $0
   b. $1
   c. $15
   d. $40

14. Which celebrity was born in Chicago?

    a. Walt Disney
    b. Will Smith
    c. Brad Pitt
    d. Meghan Markle

15. Which fast food restaurant established its first franchise location in the Chicagoland area?

    a. Burger King
    b. Wendy's
    c. McDonald's
    d. Taco Bell

16. Chicago was home of the first televised presidential debate between John F. Kennedy and Richard Nixon.

    a. True
    b. False

17. What is a common nickname for Downtown Chicago?

    a. The Work Capital of the World
    b. The Loop
    c. The City of Destiny
    d. C-Town

18. What year did Chicago's O'Hare International Airport open to commercial flights?

    a. 1969
    b. 1955
    c. 1950
    d. 1963

19. Which is not a professional sports team from Chicago?

   a. Chicago Bears
   b. Chicago Blackhawks
   c. Chicago Crushers
   d. Chicago Bulls

20. Chicago is the birthplace of soap operas.

   a. True
   b. False

QUIZ ANSWERS

1. B – Twinkies

2. A – True

3. D – It is the only river in the world that flows backward

4. C – Willis Tower

5. B – Nicotine Patch, California

6. C – Sue

7. A – True

8. B – St. Patrick's Day

9. A – Millennium Park

10. C – 1833

11. D – The Taste of Chicago

12. A – True

13. A – $0

14. A – Walt Disney

15. C – McDonald's

16. A – True

17. B – The Loop

18. B- 1955

19. C – Chicago Crushers

20. A – True

DID YOU KNOW?

1. The name "Chicago" comes from a world by the Native Americans who originated there. Chicago roughly translates to "Onion Field" or "Wild Garlic."

2. The first blood bank in the United States was established in Chicago at Cook County Hospital by Dr. Bernard Fantus in 1937.

3. Many movies were filmed in Chicago, including: *A League of their Own, Backdraft, Home Alone, Child's Play, National Lampoon's Christmas Vacation, Ferris Bueller's Day Off, Bad Boys, Sleepless in Seattle, Groundhog Day, Meet the Parents, Major League 2, While You Were Sleeping, Space Jam, Ocean's Eleven, Cheaper by the Dozen, I-Robot, Christmas with the Kranks* and *Batman Begins* … among others.

4. Chicago's famous deep-dish pizza originated in 1943 at Pizzeria Uno.

5. Chicago is home to the biggest convention center on the continent. McCormick Place has 2.6 million square feet of exhibition space.

6. Many think the nickname, "The Windy City" has to do with weather, but it actually does not. The name originated from a newspaper article back in the 1870's referring to city politicians as being "full of hot air," so it has nothing to do with wind and all to do with politics.

7. Spray paint was invented in Chicago.

8. Chicago's Western Avenue is a total length of 27.38 miles.

9. For 25 years, Oprah filmed her talk show in the West Loop of Chicago. Harpo Studios was located on Washington Blvd. and Carpenter St. The building was later demolished, and a McDonald's headquarters is now located on the site.

10. Chicago was home to one of America's first serial killers, H.H. Holmes. He was a doctor who confessed to at least 27 murders. He has also been rumored to possibly be the famed, mysterious serial killer, Jack the Ripper.

CHAPTER 17:

MR. CUB

QUIZ TIME!

1. Where was Ernie Banks born?

   a. Chicago, Illinois

   b. Angeles, California

   c. Dallas, Texas

   d. Kansas City, Missouri

2. Another one of Ernie Banks' nicknames was "Mr. Sunshine"

   a. True

   b. False

3. Ernie Banks holds the 15ᵗʰ longest consecutive games played streak in MLB history. How many games did he play consecutively from August 28, 1956, through June 22, 1961?

   a. 709

   b. 699

   c. 697

   d. 717

4. What year did Ernie Banks pass away?

    a. 2016
    b. 2015
    c. 2014
    d. 2019

5. Ernie Banks is related to which famous former NFL player?

    a. Simpson
    b. Michael Strahan
    c. Jerry Rice
    d. Lawrence Taylor

6. What nickname did his friends give Ernie when he was a teenager?

    a. Bat Boy
    b. Mr. Baseball
    c. Casper the Ghost
    d. Scooby-Doo

7. Ernie Banks was the first Cubs player to have his number retired.

    a. True
    b. False

8. What were Ernie Banks' total earnings over his 19-season career with the Cubs?

    a. $14,000,000
    b. $800,000
    c. $1,000,000
    d. $500,000

9. Where did Ernie Banks attend high school?

    a. Carroll Senior High School

    b. Lovejoy High School

    c. Highland Park High School

    d. Booker T. Washington High School

10. How did Ernie Banks die?

    a. Car Accident

    b. Cancer

    c. Heart Attack

    d. Natural Causes

11. Ernie Banks also played in the Negro Leagues. What team did he play for?

    a. Indianapolis Clowns

    b. Kansas City Monarchs

    c. New York Cubans

    d. Chicago American Giants

12. Ernie Banks was named to the MLB All-Century Team.

    a. True

    b. False

13. What does the base of Ernie Banks' statue at Wrigley Field say?

    a. "Let's Play Two!"

    b. "Mr. Cub – the greatest Cub of them all."

    c. "Ernie Banks – our most valuable player"

    d. "The only way to prove that you're a good sport is to lose."

14. How much did the Cubs buy Ernie Banks from the Kansas City Monarchs for?

    a. $50,000

    b. $100,000

    c. $5,000

    d. $10,000

15. What year did Ernie Banks retire from the game of baseball?

    a. 1969

    b. 1971

    c. 1975

    d. 1973

16. Ernie Banks' father played in the semi-pro Negro Leagues for the Dallas Green Monarchs and the Dallas Black Giants.

    a. True

    b. False

17. Ernie Banks was the first African-American _____ car dealer in the United States.

    a. Chevrolet

    b. Dodge

    c. Ford

    d. Jeep

18. Which famous actor named his son after Ernie Banks?

    a. Jeremy Piven

    b. Vince Vaughn

c. Jim Belushi

d. Bill Murray

19. Ernie Banks is known as a shortstop, but he actually played more games at first base during his 19-season career with the Cubs. How many total games did he play at first base?

    a. 1,259 games

    b. 1,300 games

    c. 1,345 games

    d. 1,125 games

20. Ernie Banks ran for office as a Republican in the 8th ward in 1963.

    a. True

    b. False

QUIZ ANSWERS

1. C – Dallas, Texas

2. A – True

3. D – 717

4. B – 2015

5. A – O.J. Simpson: Ernie's mom and O.J.'s mom were first cousins.

6. C – Casper the Ghost, because he always disappeared when there was trouble.

7. A – True

8. B – $800,000

9. D – Booker T. Washington High School

10. C – Heart attack

11. B – Kansas City Monarchs

12. A – True

13. A – "Let's Play Two!"

14. D – $10,000

15. B – 1971

16. A – True

17. C – Ford

18. D – Bill Murray

19. A – 1,259 games

20. A – True

DID YOU KNOW?

1. Ernie Banks is in a very elite club as one of only five players in the 500-home run club who hit all those home runs with one team. He joins Mickey Mantle (Yankees), Ted Williams (Red Sox), Mel Ott (Giants) and Mike Schmidt (Phillies).

2. After retirement, Ernie Banks opened a Ford dealership on the south side of Chicago, established a charity called the "Live Above and Beyond Foundation," which helps kids and the elderly with healthcare issues and became an ordained minister. He also worked for Seaway National Bank, bought a gas station and worked for an insurance company.

3. Ernie Banks is buried in Graceland Cemetery in Chicago, which is only about half a mile from Wrigley Field. His grave says, "Mr. Cub." It also has the No. 14 engraved on it and a silhouette of him batting.

4. Ernie Banks and teammate Gene Baker formed the very first all-African American middle infield in MLB history. Baker was the first to sign with the team and Banks was the first to play for the team.

5. The Cubs never made it to the playoffs during Ernie Banks' career. So, not only does he not have a World Series ring, but he never even got to play in the MLB postseason.

6. Ernie Banks served in the U.S. Army for two years. He

was drafted to serve during the Korean War. His service took him to Germany and Fort Bliss, Texas.

7. Not only did Ernie Banks excel in baseball, but he averaged 20 points per game in high school basketball and was amazing at track and field.

8. Ernie Banks was the second born among his 12 siblings. His father worked in construction and was a warehouse loader for grocery stores.

9. Mr. Cub was awarded the Presidential Medal of Freedom by President Barack Obama in 2013. Oprah Winfrey and President Bill Clinton were also honored at the ceremony.

10. Ernie Banks holds the record for most hits at Wrigley Field with 1,372.

CHAPTER 18:

FERGALICIOUS

QUIZ TIME!

1. What country was Fergie Jenkins born in?

   a. United States
   b. Canada
   c. United Kingdom
   d. Mexico

2. Fergie Jenkins attended college and played baseball at the University of Chicago.

   a. True
   b. False

3. What other sport did Fergie Jenkins excel at (besides baseball) when he was young?

   a. Golf
   b. Football
   c. Tennis
   d. Hockey

4. When was Fergie Jenkins born?

    a. December 13, 1945
    b. November 8, 1942
    c. December 13, 1942
    d. November 8, 1940

5. Fergie Jenkins' father was a chef, chauffeur and an incredible athlete. He was an amateur boxer and a semi-pro baseball player. Fergie's father played for the first all-black organized baseball team in Ontario. What was the name of that team?

    a. Ontario Royals
    b. Chatham Cubs
    c. Chatham Coloured All-Stars
    d. Ontario Otters

6. Fergie Jenkins is a member of the _____, a group of African-American pitchers who won at least 20 games in a single MLB season.

    a. African-American All-Stars
    b. Black Aces
    c. The 20s
    d. The Over-20 Club

7. Fergie Jenkins was once arrested at an airport for possession of marijuana and cocaine.

    a. True
    b. False

8. In 1974, Fergie Jenkins won the very first baseball player to win the _____, an award given each year to Canada's top athlete.

    a. Wayne Gretzky Trophy

    b. Maurice Richard Award

    c. Lou Marsh Trophy

    d. Gordie Howe Award

9. Where did Fergie Jenkins attend high school?

    a. Dorothy Gibson High School

    b. Colony High School

    c. Ontario High School

    d. Chatham Vocational High School

10. What is the title of Fergie Jenkins' autobiography?

    a. *Fergie: My Life from the Cubs to Cooperstown*

    b. *Fergie: From Chatham to Chicago*

    c. *Fergie: From Ontario to Wrigley*

    d. *Fergie: My Life from Chatham to Cooperstown*

11. How many shutouts did Fergie Jenkins throw in his career?

    a. 32

    b. 49

    c. 52

    d. 41

12. Fergie Jenkins was the first Canadian MLB player named to the National Baseball Hall of Fame.

    a. True

    b. False

13. What was Fergie Jenkins' original dream career?

    a. Auto mechanic
    b. Teacher
    c. Professional hockey player
    d. Professional golfer

14. What year was Fergie Jenkins inducted into the National Baseball Hall of Fame?

    a. 1987
    b. 2003
    c. 1995
    d. 1991

15. What year did Fergie Jenkins retire from baseball?

    a. 1980
    b. 1983
    c. 1979
    d. 1975

16. Fergie Jenkins is related to Val James, the first U.S.-born black player in the NHL.

    a. True
    b. False

17. What was Fergie Jenkin's career earned run average (ERA)?

    a. 3.69
    b. 2.98
    c. 3.34
    d. 3.40

18. How many batters did Fergie Jenkins strike out in his career?

    a. 3,412
    b. 3,001
    c. 3,333
    d. 3,192

19. Which Major League Baseball team did Fergie Jenkins NOT play for during his 19-season career?

    a. Texas Rangers
    b. Toronto Blue Jays
    c. Philadelphia Phillies
    d. Boston Red Sox

20. Fergie Jenkins played basketball for the Harlem Globetrotters during the MLB offseason from 1967 to 1969.

    a. True
    b. False

QUIZ ANSWERS

1. B – Canada

2. B – False, he did not attend college

3. D – Hockey

4. C – December 13, 1942

5. C – Chatham Coloured All-Stars

6. B – Black Aces

7. A – True

8. C – Lou Marsh Trophy

9. D – Chatham Vocational High School

10. A – *Fergie: My Life from the Cubs to Cooperstown*

11. B – 49

12. A – True

13. C – Professional hockey player

14. D – 1991

15. B – 1983

16. B – False

17. C – 3.34

18. D – 3,192

19. B – Toronto Blue Jays

20. A – True

145

DID YOU KNOW?

1. On December 17, 1979, Fergie Jenkins was made a Member of the Order of Canada for being "Canada's best-known Major League Baseball player."

2. After retirement, Fergie Jenkins ran for the Ontario Liberal Party in the 1985 Ontario General Election. He placed third. Much like Ernie Banks, he got into politics after baseball. He also worked for years with the MLB Alumni Association. In Canada, he launched the Ferguson Jenkins Charity Classic Golf Tournament. Later he founded the Fergie Jenkins Charitable Foundation, which raises funds for the Canadian Red Cross, the Special Olympics, the Canadian National Institute for the Blind, CRIED (a program for abused women) and many others.

3. On December 13, 2010, the Canada Post announced that Fergie Jenkins would be honored with his own postage stamp to celebrate Black History Month. The stamp was issued in February 2011.

4. Fergie Jenkins' mother, Delores, had ancestors who were slaves. They escaped the South through the Underground Railroad. His father's ancestors immigrated from the Barbados. Fergie Jr. is an only child.

5. In 1998, Fergie Jenkins was a pitching coach for the Texas Rangers' minor league team, the Oklahoma 89ers. He was

also the Chicago Cubs pitching coach during the 1995 and 1996 seasons.

6. Fergie's fiancée Cindy and his daughter Samantha died in a carbon monoxide poisoning murder-suicide. Cindy attached a vacuum hose to her Ford Bronco's exhaust pipe and cuddled in the back seat with Samantha until they passed. This was just two days after Fergie's 50th birthday.

7. Fergie Jenkins is often referred to as "Chatham's Favorite Son." He even lists that in his Instagram bio. Yes, at 77 years old, he is on Instagram. That shows you just how cool Fergie truly is.

8. Fergie Jenkins became the very first Commissioner of the Canadian Baseball League (CBL) in 2003. The league's championship trophy was called the Jenkins Cup, named after Fergie. The CBL only lasted one season. It consisted of eight teams: the Calgary Outlaws, the Saskatoon Legends, the Kelowna Heat, the Victoria Capitals, the London Monarchs, the Niagara Stars, the Montreal Royales and the Trois-Rivières Saints. Although no championship games were played, the Calgary Outlaws were given the Jenkins Cup for having the league's best record.

9. Fergie Jenkins was the first Canadian-born MLB player to win a Cy Young Award. Jenkins won the National League Cy Young Award in 1971.

10. Fergie Jenkins led the MLB in wins over a period of 14 seasons from 1967-1980 with 251 victories.

CONCLUSION

Learn anything new? Now you are truly the ultimate Cubs fan. Not only did you learn about the Cubs of the modern era, but you also expanded your knowledge back to the White Stockings days.

You learned about the Cubs' origins and their history, as well as where they come from. You learned about the history of their uniforms and jersey numbers, you identified some famous quotes and read some of the craziest nicknames of all time. You learned more about the ultimate bromance, Bryzzo. You learned more about Mr. Cub, Ernie Banks, and pitcher Fergie Jenkins. You absorbed some Cubs stats and recalled some of the most infamous Cubs trades and drafts. You broke down your knowledge by outfielders, infielders, pitchers and catchers. You looked back on the Cubs' World Series wins and the awards that came before, after and during them. You also learned about the Cubs' fiercest rivalries, including the crosstown White Sox and divisional Cardinals.

Every team in the MLB has a storied history, but the Cubs have a special one. Living through an 108-year World Series drought takes some dedicated fans. Being the ultimate Cubs fan takes a lot of knowledge, which you tested with this book. Whether you knew every answer or pulled a Steve Bartman on every question, you learned some of the most incredible history that the game of baseball has to offer.

The history of the Cubs represents what we all love about the game of baseball. The heart, the determination, the tough times and the unexpected moments, plus the players that inspire us and encourage us to do our best because even if you get knocked down, there is always another game and another day … even if it takes you 108 years.

With players like Anthony Rizzo, Kris Bryant and Javier Báez, the future looks bright for the Cubs. There is no doubt that this franchise will continue to be one of the most iconic sports teams in the world. The Cubbies are the heart of Chicago and represent the resilience that we should all aspire to have every day of our lives.

It's a new decade, which means there is a clean slate, ready to continue writing the history of the Chicago Cubs. The ultimate Cubs fan cannot wait to see what's to come for their lovable North Siders.

Let's hope it's not another 108 years before the next one! GO CUBS GO! Fly the W!

Made in the USA
Columbia, SC
26 March 2021